Gary

*A Memoir of the Last Year of the War for Independence,
in the Confederate States of America*
Jubal A. Early

A Southern Woman's Story
Phobe Yates Pember

Following the Greek Cross; or, Memories of the Sixth Army Corps
Thomas W. Hyde

Four Years in the Stonewall Brigade
John O. Casler

Life and Letters of Charles Russell Lowell
Edward Waldo Emerson

The generation that watched escalating sectional tensions explode into violent conflict in 1861 created an imposing published record. A struggle that killed more than six hundred thousand soldiers, subjected untold civilians to cruel material and emotional stress, and wrought enormous social and political changes prompted many individuals to chronicle their experiences. Such witnesses have much to teach modern readers, who can look to American Civil War Classics for paperback editions of important firsthand accounts. The series casts a wide net, presenting testimony from men and women, both soldiers and civilians, in the United States and the Confederacy. It presents different types of works, including sets of letters and diaries written as the war unfolded as well as memoirs and reminiscences penned from a retrospective vantage point. Historians of the period introduce the titles, placing them within the war's rich historiography and providing details about their authors. The volumes should appeal to both scholars and lay readers interested in inexpensive editions of essential texts.

GENERAL JOHN SEDGWICK

FOLLOWING THE GREEK CROSS;
OR, MEMORIES OF THE SIXTH ARMY CORPS

New introduction by Eric J. Mink

╼ THOMAS W. HYDE ╾

UNIVERSITY OF SOUTH CAROLINA PRESS

New introduction © 2005 University of South Carolina

First edition published by Houghton Mifflin, 1894

Published in Columbia, South Carolina,
by the University of South Carolina Press

Manufactured in the United States of America

09 08 07 06 05   5 4 3 2 1

Library of Congress Cataloging-in-Publication Data

Hyde, Thomas W. (Thomas Worcester), 1841–1899.
  Following the Greek Cross, or, Memories of the Sixth Army
  Corps / Thomas W. Hyde ; new introduction by Eric J. Mink.
      p. cm. — (American civil war classics)
  "First edition published by Houghton Mifflin, 1894."
  Includes bibliographical references and index.
  ISBN 1-57003-606-3 (pbk : alk. paper)
  1. Hyde, Thomas W. (Thomas Worcester), 1841–1899.
2. United States. Army. Corps, 6th (1862–1865) 3. United
States—History—Civil War, 1861–1865—Regimental histories.
4. United States—History—Civil War, 1861–1865—Personal
narratives. 5. United States. Army. Maine Infantry Regiment,
7th (1861–1864) 6. Maine—History—Civil War, 1861–1865—
Regimental histories. 7. Maine—History—Civil War, 1861–1865
—Personal narratives. 8. Soldiers—Maine—Bath—Biography.
9. Bath (Me.)—Biography. I. Title: Memories of the Sixth Army
Corps. II. Title. III. Series.
  E493.16th .H99 2005
  973.7'441—dc22

                                                    2005013312

CONTENTS

ILLUSTRATIONS

SERIES EDITOR'S PREFACE

Thomas Hyde followed the Greek cross (the corps insignia of the federal Sixth Corps) through its Civil War campaigns, serving as a staff officer at headquarters and a troop commander in the field. A series of promotions attested to Hyde's stellar performance, and eventually he received the nation's highest award for valor, the Medal of Honor, in recognition of his conduct at Antietam. His firsthand experiences, described with literary flair and in rich detail, afford students of the war an unmatched perspective on the men and operations of the sturdy organization that Hyde knew so well.

Following the Greek Cross has been long recognized as a classic and frequently cited as authoritative on its topic. It remains the most important published primary source on the Sixth Corps—one of only three corps that existed through most of the life of the Army of the Potomac. Editor Eric J. Mink has uncovered significant new evidence of the book's worth in an obscure private printing of Hyde's war-date correspondence with loved ones at home. The letters reveal that *Following the Greek Cross* is based, in most instances, directly and extensively on those contemporary documents. The origin of the memoir in that primary evidence validates even further the exalted reputation of Hyde's book.

The fresh introduction to this reissue provides valuable insight on Thomas Hyde's origins and perspectives. It also traces his considerable postwar achievements, notable among them establishment of one of the most important shipbuilding yards in North America, which remains in operation today.

Since its initial publication in 1894, *Following the Greek Cross* has been reprinted only once, in a tiny edition in 1988. This new version boasts a thorough index, which will substantially increase its utility; neither of the earlier editions had an index at all.

ROBERT K. KRICK

INTRODUCTION

The morning of May 9, 1864, dawned bright and warm across central Virginia. For four days the armies of Grant and Lee had slugged it out in the tangled thickets and open fields of Spotsylvania County. Gen. John Sedgwick, the popular commander of the Union Sixth Corps, rode down to his front lines near a fork in Brock Road, just a couple of miles north of Spotsylvania Court House. Accompanied by members of his staff, Sedgwick examined his position and looked across the open fields toward the Confederate position. Southern sharpshooters were active that morning, and bullets buzzed overhead. Sedgwick turned to Lt. Col. Thomas W. Hyde and ordered his twenty-three-year-old provost marshal to push his skirmishers out in response to the annoying early-morning fire. Upon his return, Hyde reported to his commander, who proceeded to tease him about his dangerous ride out to the forward lines. The Confederate missiles continued to kick up dust around the cluster of officers, and Sedgwick chided his men for ducking and attempting to dodge the bullets. "They couldn't hit an elephant at that distance," he said, laughing. Seconds later a shrill whistle, followed by a dull thud, interrupted the discourse, and Sedgwick slowly fell backward, the bullet having struck the general below the left eye. Hyde and the rest of the general's staff rushed to his side, but Sedgwick died instantly.[1]

In the fifteen months during which he had commanded the Sixth Corps, Sedgwick had become a beloved member of the army's leadership. The general cared for his men with an almost parental affection, and they in turn were devoted to their commander, fondly referring to him as "Uncle John." His death at Spotsylvania struck a severe blow to the morale of the Sixth Corps as well as the rest of the army. Perhaps no others felt the loss more deeply than the tight-knit family of officers who had served on his staff and shared his headquarters. "The dismay of General Sedgwick's staff was a personal feeling," wrote an officer at army headquarters, as "he was like a father to them, and they loved him really like sons."[2] One of Sedgwick's staff who particularly felt the effect of the general's death was his young provost marshal, who just moments before the tragic event had been the recipient of his commander's good-natured ribbing.

When Sedgwick assumed command of the Sixth Corps in February 1863, he personally selected Thomas W. Hyde for his staff. Hyde was an ambitious line officer in the Sixth Corps and jumped at the chance to serve at Sedgwick's headquarters. A close bond developed between the two men, to the point that, in a fit of depression shortly after Sedgwick's death, young Hyde admitted in a letter to his mother that his ambition "fled with the General's death." He added, "I do not care to stay in the service now that the General is no more."[3] Hyde overcame his grief and continued to serve in the Sixth Corps, ending the war as one of its most distinguished officers.

In the final years of his life, Hyde, inspired by his connection to Sedgwick, put pen to paper and composed a detailed history of his experiences. The result, reprinted here, is a true classic among the numerous postwar reminiscences produced by veterans of the North's premier Army of the Potomac. *Following the Greek Cross* is not merely a personal history of the war but is in many ways a story of the trials and achievements of the Sixth Corps and its beloved commander.

Thomas Worcester Hyde was born on January 15, 1841, in Florence, Italy, during his parents' yearlong honeymoon in Europe. Young Thomas was raised in his family's home in Bath, Maine, where his father, Zina, was a prominent businessman and civic leader. Through his early education in Bath's schools, he excelled in his studies, developing a strong interest in history and current events. At the age of thirteen, displaying an early penchant for adventure, he traveled alone to Boston, where he visited the Bunker Hill battlefield. Thomas continued his education at Bowdoin College in Brunswick, Maine, before accepting an offer to become a member of the first senior class of the newly formed University of Chicago. In Chicago the nineteen-year-old from Maine found himself swept up in the political debates then facing the nation.[4]

Hyde left for Illinois in the turbulent fall of 1860. A keen interest in politics, coupled with his relationship with influential friends, afforded him the opportunity to enter the tight social circles of the city. He met president-elect Abraham Lincoln at numerous parties, which served to heighten his awareness of the sectional crisis facing the nation. When not pursuing his studies, he spent time at Lincoln's office and befriended many of his associates. His constant involvement with these men influenced his emotions, and he later wrote of this time that he "felt brimful of loyalty to the government."[5] As war drew near, Hyde enlisted in a couple of different militia companies. He left Chicago in the spring of 1861, in search of active military service, and headed back to Maine to try his luck in a company from his home state.

Once back in Maine, Hyde's ambition and determination reaped its rewards. He briefly helped train and drill Bowdoin students before focusing his attention on raising his own company. Hyde succeeded in recruiting an adequate number of men to join his ranks and soon found himself being considered for a regimental office. Thomas Hyde was commissioned major of the newly formed Seventh Maine Infantry on August 21, 1861, but before the other regimental officers could join the unit, orders arrived instructing the regiment to join the army then gathering in and around Washington.[6] At the tender age of twenty, Major Hyde led his regiment for the nation's capital and the theater of war.

On March 23, 1862, the regiment boarded a steamer and, with the rest of Gen. George B. McClellan's Army of the Potomac, headed south to the Virginia Peninsula. The spring campaign of 1862 served as Hyde's baptism by fire and his first time leading troops under fire. In May the army was reorganized, and Hyde's regiment joined the newly created Sixth Corps, an association he held to the end of the war. During the intense Seven Days Campaign, the Seventh Maine saw little action. Nonetheless, Hyde gained valuable experience on his first active campaign. He routinely commanded the regiment's pickets and skirmish line, frequently conducted reconnaissances, and, as his two superiors were often ill, recurrently found himself at the head of the regiment. The young officer proved himself a responsible commander, and his superiors quickly recognized his ability to lead men.

The Battle of Antietam in September 1862 proved a turning point in Hyde's military career. Hyde once again found himself at the head of his regiment when the army entered Maryland in pursuit of Gen. Robert E. Lee. Colonel Irwin of the Forty-ninth Pennsylvania commanded the brigade to which the Seventh Maine was attached. During the day's fighting, Irwin foolishly committed his regiments piecemeal to the battle. He called on Hyde to lead his regiment in a lone attack on the Confederate lines along the Hagerstown Pike. The Seventh Maine plunged into the fields and orchard surrounding the Piper Farm and fought a desperate battle against the determined Confederates. In its solitary attack, the regiment took tremendous casualties, and Hyde came close to being captured. The young major barely managed to pull his men out of the fight and return safely to friendly lines. In the span of only a few minutes, nearly half of the regiment became casualties. The foolish order to attack incensed Hyde, but he obeyed and fought as well as could be expected, and his efforts did not go unnoticed by his superiors.

Thirty years later Hyde received the country's highest honor for his role at Antietam. Gen. William F. Smith, his division commander in the battle, recommended him for the Medal of Honor and wrote that he was "struck with the gallantry of the colonel [major] and the regiment" in an attack that had originated from the inspiration "of the brigade commander which like many other inspirations on the part of ignorant leaders led to unfortunate results." In his endorsement of Hyde, Sixth Corps commander Gen. William B. Franklin proclaimed the major's "conduct in bringing back his regiment . . . an act of distinguished bravery, and so told him." Franklin added, "I think it deserving of the recognition accorded to acts of special bravery."[7]

The Maryland Campaign further cemented Hyde's reputation as a brave and dependable officer. As his stock rose, so too did his desire to obtain higher office. Hyde had a rocky relationship with his lieutenant colonel; the major chafed under his command, wanting and expecting promotion. "I should now have little diffidence in taking command of a Brigade," he boasted to his mother in early October, "and will have one before I am two years older . . . I am trying for a Brigadier Generalship but may get a high staff appointment that will be permanent."[8] Much reduced following Antietam, the Seventh Maine was sent home on leave. Back in Maine, Hyde lobbied hard for one of the new regiments being raised by the governor, but his efforts proved unsuccessful. In late January 1863, he returned to the army and, much to his satisfaction, managed to secure a staff position with General Smith, then commanding the Army of the Potomac's Left Grand Division.[9] This appointment proved temporary, for a week later Gen. Joseph Hooker abolished the grand divisions. For a couple of weeks, Hyde served as acting inspector general of the Sixth Corps, and on February 20 he was officially appointed Sedgwick's provost marshal.[10] Hyde still longed to serve at the head of a Maine regiment, but until that chance came he was content to find himself among the military family that served at corps headquarters.

A position on staff was an enviable one. The duties of a staff officer often included mundane paperwork and tirelessly working around the clock delivering orders. The elevated position, however, provided more freedom, as he informed his mother. He wrote, "[It] brings me in contact with new phases of men and gives new phases of duty." Although he spent most of his time behind the lines shuffling paper, Hyde managed to find his way onto the battlefields that summer. At Fredericksburg in May he participated in the storming of Marye's Heights and rejoined the Seventh Maine in an attack along Smith's Run. At Gettysburg he preceded the Sixth Corps to Gettysburg and guided the command to the battlefield. At Mine Run in November, Hyde received orders to accompany the troops in a planned assault on the Confederate lines but expressed relief when, at the last minute, the order to attack was suspended. His attention to duty and coolness under fire that year were rewarded in December with a promotion to the rank of lieutenant colonel.[11]

The opening of the 1864 campaign once again launched Hyde into the midst of the fighting. In the Wilderness, he participated in the attacks north of the Orange Turnpike and on the second day of the battle helped to rally elements of the Sixth Corps that broke under Confederate general John B. Gordon's flank attack. Two days later the armies faced each other near Spotsylvania Court House, where he lost the benevolent Sedgwick. The kindly commander of the Sixth Corps had taken Hyde under his wing, fostered his ambition, and furthered his career in the army. "Surely those of us who made his military family then," he wrote, "can look back upon no greater privilege, no more lasting recollection than being permitted to enjoy his confidence and appreciate his simple greatness" (172–73).

With a heavy heart, Hyde stayed at his post and continued to serve the Sixth Corps under its new commander, Gen. Horatio G. Wright. From Spotsylvania through Cold Harbor and on to Petersburg, Hyde passed through the spring battles. In July the corps was ordered to Washington to help repel Jubal Early's advance on the capital. Hyde became increasingly concerned about his former command at this time. The Seventh Maine numbered slightly fewer than two hundred men and was without a regimental officer. He persuaded Wright to relieve him of his staff duties and allow him to return to the regiment. The general consented, and as they chased Early back into the Shenandoah Valley, Hyde once again exercised temporary command of the Maine regiment. As before, his placement there was short lived. In late August the regiment's term of service expired, and Hyde and his men received orders to head home.[12]

In three years of war Hyde had gained for himself an enviable reputation and much experience as a battlefield commander. He witnessed his share of bloodshed and suffered the loss of many close friends, but his desire to lead at the head of a Maine regiment remained unwavering. He immediately set out for Augusta and petitioned the governor for command of the First Maine Veteran Volunteers, an infantry regiment comprised of those men in the Seventh Maine who reenlisted, supplemented by similar companies from the Fifth and Sixth Maine regiments. In October his long-awaited commission arrived, and once again he left home for the war.[13]

Hyde arrived in Washington on October 17, unaware that his regiment was then embroiled in the pivotal fighting along Cedar Creek in the Shenandoah Valley. He arrived two days following the engagement and immediately reported for duty. Throughout his service Hyde coveted a colonelcy in a Maine regiment, but upon his arrival in Winchester he discovered, much to his surprise, that he was the ranking officer in his brigade and therefore took command of not one but six regiments. The responsibilities appealed to Hyde, and the ambition and drive that had seemed to wane in the months following Sedgwick's death returned. Writing to his mother a couple of weeks after his arrival in Virginia, Hyde informed her, "I am feeling very proud and ambitious and have kept all my good resolutions thus far. . . . I don't want to come home again until I wear a star."[14]

Hyde spent the fall of 1864 in the valley attached to Sheridan's army, but in December the Sixth Corps was ordered to rejoin the Army of the Potomac around Petersburg. The winter passed in relative inactivity, but that was shattered on the morning of March 25 when Confederate general John B. Gordon launched an attack against the Union fortifications, gaining early success at Fort Stedman. Along his section of the line, Hyde handled his brigade with consummate skill, and in the Union counterattack the Sixth Corps was able to advance and seize the forward Confederate picket line. This advantage proved instrumental to the Union plans in the coming week.

The seizure of the picket line by the Sixth Corps closed the gap between the opposing defenses to about half a mile, a perfect location for launching an attack. On April 2, the Sixth Corps arrayed itself in a wedge-shaped assault alignment behind Fort Fisher. Hyde's brigade took position in the second line of the wedge. At the appointed hour, the formation sprang forward, sweeping the Confederate pickets out of the way. Over the Confederate works and into their rear the Sixth Corps pushed, on to the Boydton Plank Road, Hatcher's Run, and the outskirts of the city. The Confederate lines had been breached, the ten-month Confederate defense of Petersburg unraveled, and Richmond was doomed. In the attack, Hyde performed admirably and was duly recognized for his action, earning recommendation for a brevet promotion to brigadier general, which was confirmed a few months later.[15]

The Petersburg lines had been broken, but Lee's army remained on the move. In the final days of the war, Hyde's brigade participated in the pursuit of Lee. Three times his regiments were put in position for a fight, but each time the opportunity passed. The Army of Northern Virginia surrendered on April 9, but Hyde and the rest of the Sixth Corps were not there to witness the end. Instead they were ordered to Danville, where Hyde presided as military governor and paroled prisoners. The Sixth Corps' duties forced the men to miss the Grand Review of the Army of the Potomac in Washington, but on June 8, a special review was held for the men who followed the Greek cross.

Marching triumphantly down Pennsylvania Avenue, flags fluttering in the breeze, the Sixth Corps made an impressive sight. Standing along the parade route was Gen. Joshua L. Chamberlain, a division commander in the Fifth Corps and, like Hyde, a former Bowdoin College student and native of Maine. As the Sixth Corps swung into view, Chamberlain admired its formation and reflected on the unit's achievements and sacrifices. The corps was well known throughout the army for its procession of stalwart commanders, Chamberlain thought, but above all else "as we know them best, the men of Sedgwick." As the First Maine marched into view, Chamberlain noticed the young officer riding at the head of the brigade. "Commanding it the young general, Tom Hyde," he later wrote, "favorite in all the army, prince of staff officers, gallant commander, alert of sense, level of head, sweet of soul."[16]

The fighting over, his friends and superiors urged
Hyde to pursue a career in the postwar army. General
Wright petitioned the secretary of war that Hyde be
given a brigade command in the reorganized army.
"There is no more promising officer or better brigade
commander than Col. Hyde," Wright wrote in his
endorsement. Hyde had entered the army straight
out of school and knew no other vocation. Although
the thought of a military career sounded appealing,
after four years of war he was eager to get home. On
June 28, 1865, Lt. Col. Thomas Hyde was mustered
out of federal service.[17]

Hyde left for the war in 1861 a young, enthusiastic
schoolboy but returned a responsible leader of men.
His wartime experience handling men and bearing
responsibility prepared him for a highly successful
civilian career. A few months after returning to Bath,
Hyde purchased a small iron foundry that manufactured cast-iron stoves and parts for ship machinery.
He quickly expanded the business when he patented
the Hyde windlass and added both steam and hand
windlasses to his inventory. In 1884 Hyde incorporated under the name Bath Iron Works, Limited. Four
years later, he purchased another iron foundry and
began to pursue the possibility of turning Bath into a
shipbuilding community. Hyde's vision was achieved
on February 28, 1890, when the Bath Iron Works received its first government contract for the construc-
tion of two 190-foot steel gunboats. Following on the
heels of these contracts came orders for civilian craft,

such as yachts and merchant steamers. From the small iron foundry first purchased by Hyde grew one of the region's largest shipyards, which continues today to provide warships for the country's defense.[18]

Hyde was as successful in his private and public life as in his business ventures. In 1866 he married his childhood friend and sweetheart, Annie Hayden. The first of six children followed a year later, a son whom the couple christened John Sedgwick in honor of Hyde's fallen commander. Hyde pursued a successful political career, serving in the Maine state senate for three terms and being elected mayor of Bath twice. He also spent eight years as a member of the board of visitors of the United States Military Academy in West Point, New York.[19]

In the fall of 1899, Hyde's health began to decline. He moved to the Hotel Chamberlain in Old Point Comfort, Virginia, hoping that a milder climate would improve his health. On November 14, 1899, surrounded by his family, Thomas W. Hyde died of Bright's disease. His death was a blow to the town of Bath. The local newspaper referred to Hyde as "Bath's best loved son" and mourned the loss of "her greatest benefactor . . . without which Bath would have died long ago." Four days later his body returned to Bath, and with it came many of his former comrades who had served alongside him during the war. Martin T. McMahon, J. Ford Kent, and Charles Whittier, all of whom had served with Hyde on Sedgwick's staff, were present, as were Joshua Chamberlain and Holman Melcher of the Twentieth Maine. "The funeral," wrote the editor of the *Bath Independent,* "was in all respects the most impressive that has taken place in Bath." Hyde's remains were laid to rest in Oak Grove Cemetery.[20]

While Hyde was relentless in his business pursuits after the war, he never forgot the four years he spent in the army. He became a member of the Military Order of the Loyal Legion of the United States, a fraternal organization of former Union officers, of which he was commander of the Maine commandery for many years. At their periodic meetings, members delivered speeches on various wartime subjects, frequently providing their own personal accounts of military events. Hyde contributed a number of papers to these proceedings, and it was probably while composing them that he was first struck with the idea of writing his memoirs.[21]

Following the Greek Cross was released in 1894 by Houghton, Mifflin and Company. It met with a favorable response from the public, and the book enjoyed a second printing the following year. Reviews in the press praised Hyde's memoirs, heralding his frank recounting of life in the army. "He knows what people wish to hear, when a soldier sets about narrating his adventures," opined the *Atlantic Monthly,* "and thus this book ... is a capital reproduction of army life in its common experience."[22] An assessment in the *New*

York Times also focused on the book's valuable description of soldier life, stating that "it is to be chiefly considered as one of the most fascinating records of personal experience in the war of the rebellion ever published." This reviewer further noted that Hyde's opinions were "freely expressed, and ... sometimes startling" and suggested that "Gen. Hyde's book will be seriously considered by future historians."[23]

Historians have found much value in Hyde's reminiscence, and it continues to be one of the most cited sources for information on the Army of the Potomac and the war in the east. In their 1967 *Civil War Books: A Critical Bibliography,* prominent Civil War historians Allan Nevins, James I. Robertson Jr., and Bell I. Wiley referred to the book as "an excellent memoir."[24] More recently, David J. Eicher called it "an excellent work that retains its value today."[25] Continued interest in the book prompted a small-run reprint of the volume in 1988 by Olde Soldier Books of Gaithersburg, Maryland. While historians still enjoy Hyde's retelling of the events he witnessed, his memoir has always lacked an important element to any historical narrative. With this most recent printing of *Following the Greek Cross,* the University of South Carolina Press adds an index, an important element missing from all previous editions.

Memoirs and reminiscences can at times fall prey to a cloudy memory. The more time between the events and their recordation, the more room there is for error or confusion. *Following the Greek Cross* was written thirty years after the war, during a period when the author was building an industrial empire and his mind was greatly distracted by business concerns. Yet Hyde recounted his experiences and adventures with amazing accuracy. He was aided in composing his memoirs by the retention of a series of wartime letters and correspondence with his family. When comparing these letters to his memoirs, it is quite evident that Hyde relied heavily upon them. Some sections of his published work are taken almost verbatim from this correspondence. There are, however, a few discrepancies, most of which are of little consequence; but his description of Gettysburg appears greatly exaggerated.

In recounting his involvement of the third day at Gettysburg, Hyde apparently injected himself into the story more than his actual participation warranted. He tells of lunching with General Meade and other officers prior to the Confederate assault on Cemetery Ridge. He further states that he felt an attack was imminent and warned the army commander of that fact. Hyde describes the action and tells of riding down to the scene afterward and seeing the mortally wounded Confederate general Lewis Armistead. Hyde paints a very vivid description of these events; however, in a lengthy letter, dated September 6, 1863, to his mother, in which he detailed his participation at Gettysburg, Hyde mentioned none of these things. In fact, he told her that just prior to the attack he had gone back to the wagons and caught a few minutes of sleep, only to be awakened by the bombardment. "This was the prelude to the main attack on our center," he informed his mother, "which I did not see."[26] Perhaps Hyde got caught up in the postwar romanticism surrounding the battle and opted to create for himself a larger role in the engagement. Whatever the reason, the chapter on Gettysburg appears to be the only portion of the book where he took literary liberties. The remainder of his memoir proves honest and truthful.

The most useful portions of his text are Hyde's dramatic details of the many battles he participated in, Gettysburg excepted. His recounting of Antietam is wonderfully written, with its painstaking minutiae on his regiment's disastrous attack and Hyde's own personal adventure on the battlefield. Second Fredericksburg receives thorough coverage; Hyde's account of that battle remains today one of the chief sources of information in helping to reconstruct the actions along Smith's Run. The horrors of the Wilderness come alive in a graphic description of the death of a soldier whose brains were sprayed across Hyde's face. The prolonged fight at Spotsylvania receives detailed attention, and Hyde's interaction with many of the army's officers is retold with wonderful clarity. *Following the Greek Cross* is the type of memoir that military historians dream of, chock full of striking detail and wonderfully quotable passages, all written in a compelling and lively style.

From his elevated position as a staff officer and brigade commander, Hyde came in frequent contact with many of the Army of the Potomac's leaders and key personalities. In the text, the reader will find many useful and entertaining descriptions and assessments of these men. George Meade, Hyde remembered, "in his well-worn uniform, splashed with mud, with his glasses, and his nervous and earnest air, looked more like a learned pundit than a soldier" (140). Hyde felt that the Army of the Potomac was never very enthusiastic about Grant but "forgave the cruel and unnecessary losses they sustained under him on account of the results attained" (180). The much-maligned William B. Franklin was, in Hyde's estimation, "cool and brave, and of great ability" (116). Henry W. Halleck, on the other hand, Hyde described as a "military crank" (140). While many important figures appear within these pages, Sedgwick looms largest as the man for whom Hyde reserves his greatest praise. A "lion in battle, but with the harness off, gentle as a woman, unselfish as a saint" was Hyde's estimation of his chief (172). "I look on it now as my proudest distinction," he admitted, "that I was enabled to serve with him while he lived" (123).

Historians have wrongly attempted to categorize *Following the Greek Cross* as a unit history of the

Sixth Corps.[27] That was not Hyde's intention. His intention was simply to convey his own views and experiences. In the process, however, he effectively documented the role of the Sixth Corps. Hyde served exclusively with this illustrious organization from its formation in 1862 through to the end in 1865, and as a line and staff officer he participated in nearly all of its engagements. The result is that his memoirs present an outline for the service of the corps, of which he was immensely proud. From the highest officer to the lowliest private, Hyde wrote with great affection of the soldiers who fought and died within its ranks. This simple yet impressive memoir presents the record of one man's service in the war but also serves as a testimony to the many men who served under the banner of the Sixth Corps and followed the Greek cross.

NOTES TO INTRODUCTION

1. Martin T. McMahon, "The Death of General Sedgwick," in *Battles and Leaders of the Civil War,* ed. Robert Underwood Johnson and Clarence Clough Buel (New York: Century, 1888), 4:175.

2. George R. Agassiz, ed., *Meade's Headquarters, 1863–1865: Letters of Colonel Theodore Lyman from the Wilderness to Appomattox* (Boston: Atlantic Monthly Press, 1922), 108.

3. Thomas W. Hyde, *Civil War Letters of General Thomas W. Hyde* (privately printed, 1933), 132. This rare volume was published by Hyde's grandson. It contains many of Hyde's wartime letters to his mother and sister. The letters now reside in the Thomas W. Hyde Papers, George J. Mitchell Department

of Special Collections and Archives, Bowdoin College, Brunswick, Maine.

4. Madelyn Phillips O'Neill, "Notes on the Hyde Family" (manuscript in the Thomas W. Hyde Papers, George J. Mitchell Department of Special Collections and Archives, Bowdoin College, Brunswick, Maine), 20.

5. Thomas W. Hyde to Annie Hayden, no date, quoted in O'Neill, "Notes on the Hyde Family," 20.

6. Thomas W. Hyde's military service in the Seventh Maine Infantry is documented in his Compiled Service Records in "Records of the Adjutant General's Office, 1780s–1917," RG 94, National Archives, Washington, D.C.

7. Thomas W. Hyde's receipt of the Medal of Honor is documented in his Medal of Honor file and can be found in "Records of the Adjutant General's Office, 1780s–1917," RG 94, entry 496, National Archives, Washington, D.C.

8. Hyde, *Civil War Letters of General Thomas W. Hyde,* 55.

9. Ibid., 60.

10. Thomas W. Hyde, compiled service record, Seventh Maine Infantry, National Archives, Washington, D.C.

11. Ibid.

12. Ibid.

13. Thomas W. Hyde's military service in the First Maine Veteran Infantry is documented in his compiled service records in "Records of the Adjutant General's Office, 1780s–1917," RG 94, National Archives, Washington, D.C.

14. Hyde, *Civil War Letters of General Thomas W. Hyde,* 149.

15. Thomas W. Hyde, compiled service record, First Maine Veteran Infantry, National Archives, Washington, D.C. Although no longer in the army, in 1867 Hyde was recommended for a promotion to the rank of brevet major general. He never received that promotion, but documents relating to the nomination can be found on microfilm M1064, rolls 334, 433, and 435, National Archives, Washington, D.C.

16. Joshua L. Chamberlain, *The Passing of the Armies* (New York: G. P. Putnam's Sons, 1915), 360–61.

17. Documents pertaining to Thomas W. Hyde's recommendation for postwar duty in the army are on microfilm M1064, roll 164, National Archives, Washington, D.C.

18. Garnett Laidlaw Eskew, *Cradle of Ships* (New York: G. P. Putnam's Sons, 1958), 33–37; William Avery Baker, *A Maritime History of Bath, Maine and the Kennebec River Region* (Bath: Maritime Museum, 1973), 2:697–705. On May 5, 1943, the New England Shipbuilding Corporation launched the *Thomas W. Hyde,* a freighter and limited troop carrier Liberty Ship named in honor of the man who had done so much for Maine's shipbuilding industry. Walter W. Jaffee, *The Liberty Ships from A (A. B. Hammond) to Z (Zona Gale)* (Palo Alto, Calif.: Glencannon Press, 2004), 297.

19. George Thomas Little, comp., *Genealogical and Family History of the State of Maine* (New York: Lewis Historical Publishing Co., 1909), 3:1374–76.

20. *Bath Independent,* November 18 and 25, 1899.

21. Little, *Genealogical and Family History of the State of Maine,* 3:1375. Only one of Hyde's papers reached publication. It dealt with Gettysburg and is nearly identical in many ways to the chapter that appears in his memoirs. Thomas W. Hyde, "Recollections of the Battle of Gettysburg," in *War Papers Read before the Commandery of the State of Maine, Military Order of the Loyal Legion of the United States* (Portland, Maine: Thurston, 1898), 1:191–206. In a speech before the Maine commandery in 1917, Brevet Maj. Henry Burrage suggested that other papers Hyde delivered before the organization were incorporated into his memoirs. Henry S. Burrage, "Historical Address at the Fiftieth Anniversary of the Maine Commandery, December 7, 1916," in *Vermont War Papers and Miscellaneous States Papers and Addresses for Military Order of the Loyal Legion of the United States* (Wilmington, N.C.: Broadfoot, 1994), 221.

22. "Comments on New Books," *Atlantic Monthly,* June 1895, 847.

23. "The Boy Brigadier," *New York Times,* October 21, 1894.

24. Allan Nevins, James I. Robertson Jr., and Bell I. Wiley, eds., *Civil War Books: A Critical Bibliography* (Baton Rouge: Louisiana State University Press, 1967), 1:109.

25. David J. Eicher, *The Civil War in Books: An Analytical Bibliography* (Urbana: University of Illinois Press, 1997), 356.

26. Hyde, *Civil War Letters of General Thomas W. Hyde,* 100.

27. In his massive and thorough compilation of Civil War literature, New York librarian and bibliophile Charles E. Dornbusch listed Hyde's memoir under the category of corps histories. C. E. Dornbush, *Military Bibliography of the Civil War* (New York: New York Public Library, 1972), 3:90. David J. Eicher described the book as "essentially a unit history of the 6th Corps." Eicher, *The Civil War in Books,* 356.

PREFACE TO THE 1894 EDITION

As a preface should properly be the last thing written, after reading this book again it seems to me that this preface should be an apology for personality. And yet I should like to read a book written in the same vein by some officer of the Revolutionary army. The personal narratives, scant as they are, of the Napoleonic campaigns are of rare interest: so perhaps some day my apology may be received, and I be wholly pardoned for putting upon the public what was originally intended for my children and neighbors. We old soldiers have flooded the country with our kind of literature, and we have been reasonably ready at all times to explain about the war; but it is not for long before our voices will be silent, our pens as rusty as our swords, and our pensions cancelled. Bear with us but a little longer, O gracious Public.

THOMAS W. HYDE

Bath, Maine, July, 1894

FOLLOWING THE
GREEK CROSS

FOLLOWING THE GREEK CROSS.

CHAPTER I.

> " Our chief of men, who through a cloud,
> Not of war only, but detractions rude,
> Guided by faith and matchless fortitude."
>
> MILTON.

WHETHER it is worth while to preserve the personal recollections of those who lived and acted during the stirring days of 1860 to 1865, however humble may have been their position, is a question difficult for me to consider in an unbiased frame of mind. When we remember the large part of the population of the United States who have been born and have entered into active life since then, as well as the great numbers of our youth growing into manhood, it may, perhaps, seem probable that they might feel an interest in what an older generation then thought and did while the country was in the throes of the most gigantic war of modern times. Such an interest is best aroused by personal narration, however difficult it is to one who would prefer to be impersonal. A history of those times, now hardly to be called recent, is yet to be written, and when it is written it will stand, like the line of battle, behind personal narratives, the skirmishers which precede it.

In the fall of 1860, many signs and omens of a coming dissolution of the Union were visible, but boys of eighteen and nineteen were not much impressed by them.

Having been invited at that time by the Hon. J. Young Scammon, of Chicago, to make a part of the first senior class of the University of Chicago, a new institution in which he was deeply interested, I left Bowdoin College to spend a year in what seemed to us then almost the Western wilds. There were three of us in this class and we had the undivided attention of President Burroughs and some able professors. As our recitation hours were from nine to two o'clock, each of us had nearly two hours of personal attention. We usually followed this by an hour in the Chicago gymnasium, to which I attribute the sturdy health which enabled me afterward to brave four years of campaigning with but one day of hospital. The Chicago University was a Baptist college, and after some years of usefulness fell into a moribund condition. It has lately received an enormous gift from John D. Rockefeller, and will in time be one of the greatest seats of learning in the country. Chicago at that time had about one hundred thousand population, nearly seventy per cent. of which were of foreign birth.

The presidential campaign, which ended in the election of Mr. Lincoln, was going on. Night after night processions of Wide Awakes, many thousands in numbers, thronged its streets. Immense audiences at the Wigwam listened to the stirring oratory of the best speakers of the day. I remember best the powerful speeches of Owen Lovejoy, the greatest stump orator I ever heard. He would hold spellbound for two hours at a time nine thousand people in this vast hall, tearing his coat off and then his vest and cravat in the excitement of his invectives against slavery, though never alluding to the fact that but a short time before his brother had been shot by a pro-slavery mob.

Before the convention had declared the will of the Republican party, Seward seemed to be the popular candidate, especially among the young people ; though some of us from Maine talked all we could for the Hon. William Pitt Fessenden, our lamented Senator. Very few of us who had come from the East had heard of Mr. Lincoln, but when he was nominated, the perusal of his great speeches, and the many traditions extant of his political successes, taught us what kind of a man he was.

The first time I had the pleasure of seeing

him was at a party given at the residence of
Hon. N. B. Judd on Michigan Avenue. I lately
saw this same house still standing. The great
fire almost reached it. As I went upstairs, Mr.
Lincoln was leaning against a door in the gentlemen's dressing-room, with his hands crossed
behind his back, holding up the long tails of a
very long dress-coat, and telling stories to several gentlemen who were gathered around. All
who came in joined the party, and it was with
difficulty that their ladies could get them to go
downstairs. I tried to remember some of these
stories, which seemed inimitably funny at the
time, but was unable to catch them or carry
them away. I have always thought since that
Mr. Lincoln possessed the power of inventing
stories as he went along, which were intended to
illustrate whatever thought he wished to convey,
and did so in the most vivid way possible.
During that winter I saw Mr. Lincoln many
times, as he often stopped at Mr. Scammon's,
where I lived, when he came to Chicago.

Mr. Lincoln and Mr. Hamlin, the vice-presi-
dent elect, met each other for the first time at
Mr. Scammon's house. I saw them introduced,
and it was with a deep look of interest that each
regarded the other. Then they retired for a
long personal consultation. When Mr. Hamlin
went away, Mr. Lincoln remarked, " Well, Ham-

lin is n't half so black as he is painted, is he, Scammon ? " At that time, the story was current at the South that our Maine statesman was a mulatto, on account of his rich, dark complexion.

When the Illinois Legislature of that winter was in session, Mr. Scammon was a member of the House, and invited me to visit him in Springfield for three weeks. The night after my arrival, I went to the party given by Mr. and Mrs. Lincoln at their Springfield home just before they closed it and went to the hotel, where we were living, to board until his departure for Washington to be inaugurated. The house was not very large, as I remember it, but the party of guests was enormous. People from all parts of Illinois were there, and the guests passed through the rooms shaking hands with Mr. and Mrs. Lincoln, who were surrounded by a bevy of beautiful girls from Kentucky, and then most of them passed out and went to the reception Governor Yates was giving the same night at the Capitol.

Becoming acquainted with Ellsworth, afterwards colonel of the Fire Zouaves and killed at Alexandria ; Mr. Hay and Mr. Nicolay, who were law students in Mr. Lincoln's office, and since his biographers, I often went there in the afternoon and assisted them in looking over his

mail, which at that time filled several large
baskets. Many packages would come with letters, some containing negro doll babies, some,
dead rattlesnakes, and various tokens of that
description from angry Southerners. When-
ever a box looked particularly suspicious, we
used to soak it in water, fearing some infernal
machine. Mr. Lincoln received daily in his
office many people from all parts of the country,
and it was very entertaining to me to hear the
bright way in which he would receive them, and
the skillful way he met the office-seekers. Of
all the witty things I then heard him say, only
one remains in my memory to-day. Dr. Small,
the leading homœopathic physician of Chicago,
who weighed nearly three hundred pounds, was
presented to him. I remember Mr. Lincoln's
taking him by the hand, turning him round,
looking him over, and saying, " Small, Small?
we have a man down in old Virginia that
they call Wise; " referring to Governor Wise,
who had for some time been acting in an entirely
different manner from what his name indicated.
Just before the day came for Mr. Lincoln to
take his departure for Washington, many distinguished people came to the hotel where we
lived and many others who afterward became
distinguished. One day I was introduced to
Captain Pope and Major Hunter, of the regular

army, afterward commanders of armies. Many stories were rife of the great dangers to be met in the journey to Washington by Mr. Lincoln's party. Mrs. Lincoln was especially anxious upon this point, and almost in a state of nervous prostration. Mr. Lincoln was kind enough to invite me to join the party, but circumstances forbade my going. Our late distinguished Minister to England, a boy of about sixteen, was too young to realize his father's position, but I remember well what a universal favorite he was with all, and he certainly has continued to be a universal favorite ever since. Ellsworth was a black-eyed, handsome, enthusiastic boy. He had recently taken his company of Chicago Zouaves upon an Eastern tour, and had been received in all the principal cities with great applause, as it was the best drilled military company ever organized. They were all athletes, trained in the Chicago gymnasium, and their evolutions were novel and surprising.

Not long after the departure of Mr. Lincoln for Washington, the rumors and fears of war between the sections came thicker and faster, and when Mr. Lincoln issued his call for seventy-five thousand troops, the Chicago Zouaves undertook to raise a regiment, of which I had the honor to be a private in Company D. As I recollect it, the first three companies, A, B, and

C, were accepted, and went off to Cairo, leaving the rest of us very much disgusted at home, though we gave them a rousing send-off at the station. We might have easily raised then all the men needed for the war, as nearly all young men were full of patriotism. When the news came of the attack on the Massachusetts troops in the streets of Baltimore, we were still further excited, and I told my comrades I would give five years of my life to march a regiment through that city. The fulfillment of the wish came with almost alarming promptness, for only four months later, at the head of the 7th Maine Volunteers, I marched the whole length of Baltimore Street to the inspiring strains of Yankee Doodle. Events were hurrying swiftly, and boys aged very rapidly then, but I can even now hardly realize that the war was fought mostly by boys of eighteen to twenty-five years of age. But those who were so ardently seeking to serve their country had very little idea what was meant. Some of them had learned to read well enough to become excited over the bulletins of victory during the Mexican war, and others had fathers or grandfathers who had served against England in the war of 1812, either by land or sea. The great-grandfathers of very many of us had fought the English in the Revolution, or the French and Indians during the early settle-

ments, for then every ablebodied man from
Eastport to Portsmouth was a soldier. Traditions and tales of martial deeds still had an in-
fluence on that young generation ; so it was not
difficult to excite the warlike spirit, especially
after the stars and stripes were fired upon at
Fort Sumter.

About this time at a dinner party at Mr.
Scammon's, several Illinois statesmen, among
them Hon. Lyman Trumbull, being present, all
expressed the opinion that the seventy-five thousand men raised by Mr. Lincoln would march
through to the Gulf of Mexico with little difficulty. I modestly said that when a child I had
seen five thousand splendid militia under arms
at Charleston, South Carolina, receive Generals
Quitman and Shields on their return from the
Mexican war, and that the militia of the South
would alone require many more than seventy-
five thousand men to overcome them. The distinguished statesmen deigned no reply, but looked
at me as if I was very impertinent, and perhaps
I was.

All the West, as well as Chicago, was now at
fever heat of patriotism, and many regiments
were forming to march to defend the Union
when Mr. Lincoln should call for more troops.
Among these was a regiment to be commanded
by the Hon. Owen Lovejoy, called the Yates

Phalanx, in which I enlisted, but hearing of the departure of the 3d Maine which contained two Bath companies and many of my friends and schoolmates, to the seat of war, and as the college authorities permitted me to take my degree, I concluded not to wait for commencement, but to go home and join some Maine regiment.

CHAPTER II.

"And blessed is a country with stout hearts like these,
   The tramp of her armies is swelling the breeze;
   They rush to her rescue, their lives freely give,
   'T were better to die than in bondage to live."

MOSES OWEN.

ON arriving home from the West, after a long
journey by rail in cars whose discomfort we have
almost forgotten, I found a lull in the war fever,
and a general opinion that it was to be a short
affair. After some weeks at Bowdoin College,
where I taught the students the Zouave drill and
directed as skirmishers many future generals
and colonels down Main Street to capture the
Topsham bridge, I went home for the last vaca-
tion, sadly feeling that my chance would never
come. One day while working about the house,
an acquaintance drove by and called out, "Our
army has been badly beaten at Bull Run." Now
or never seemed the time to go to war, as more
troops must be wanted. That afternoon Sam Fessenden, who was the son of the Senator, and was
killed at Manassas, George O. McLellan, soon to
be killed at Yorktown, and George Morse, now
living, joined me, and as there was no recruiting
office in town, we thought the next thing to do

was to be sworn into the United States service;
so we went to Lawyer Fred D. Sewall and were
solemnly sworn into the service of the United
States, and I took the next train for Augusta to
obtain papers to recruit a company.   Meeting
H. S. Hagar, of Richmond, on the train, bound
on the same errand, we agreed to join forces, and
in a day or two a recruiting office was opened,
and yellow handbills were distributed as follows:

ONE CHANCE MORE.

A few good men wanted for the Bath Company of
the 7th Regiment.   Pay and sustenance to commence immediately.

$15.00 A MONTH.

$22.00 bounty and $100.00 when mustered out of
service.   Apply at their recruiting office, opposite J.
M. Gookin's store, Front Street.

BATH, MAINE, Aug. 6, '61.

The company was called the Harding Zouaves.
Col. E. K. Harding, of Bath, then quarter-
master-general of the State, had a rare faculty
of encouraging young men and winning their
admiration, and to his kindly efforts and judicious advice I owed much then and afterward.
Praise judiciously bestowed from those we look
up to is so rare that I have preserved the memory of his kind words now many a year since;
in sorrow we said, " Peace go with him."

The first accession gained in my new office, which had for furniture one chair and a table, was what we would now call a tramp; the word was unknown then. He had but one eye, and claimed to have served in the British army; so we looked on him with a certain reverence his appearance never could have claimed, and gave him of the fat of the land. He soon deserted, but he had fulfilled his mission: he had given us hope of success, so his brief tarry in the colonies was of some avail. But men began to come in and were sent to Augusta daily, and soon I followed them, anxious to taste the sweets of command. On the long, beautiful slopes between the State House and the river, Sibley tents were pitched. They were like an Indian tepee in shape. Hundreds of men of the 7th Regiment were already in camp, and I soon found Company D, and was received by Lieutenant Morse with all the honors, and a supper that no one can appreciate who has not eaten beans baked in a hole in the ground. Soon after supper it began to rain, and as our tents, though floored with planed boards and containing plenty of blankets, had no straw, it struck me that it was a cruel hardship to treat brave men so, and I mustered the company and marched them off to the nearest hotel and put them up at my own expense. I then invited the lieutenants to sleep in camp with me, so we could inure ourselves to campaigning; but with the novelty and excitement we sat up and told stories till it was time to go the grand rounds, which thrilling peace-time military ceremony impressed us deeply. Before morning the rain ceased, but not the mosquitoes, and when the company sauntered leisurely down to breakfast they saw their officers looking as if they had been up all night watching with the sick.

The next day arms were issued to us: Winsor rifles, with plenty of brass trimmings to keep clean, and sabre bayonets. Very proud we were of them, and when we came to use them we found they shot pretty straight. Cumbersome as the sabre bayonets were, they were good to dig shelter with, and several times I have seen their long leveled lines carry consternation to the gray-clothed foe.

Fresh from my Zouave training, I soon had Company D in shape, and I loved every man in it. The delight of a first command was on me, and even now I can see the faces of all, from the tall man on the right to little Charlie Price, the shortest, on the left. I see them just as they looked then, enthusiastic and boyish, but of those eighty most are now with the silent majority. Four years in the 7th Maine did not prove favorable to longevity. They were going

LIEUTENANT-COLONEL T. W. HYDE

to the call of duty, to brave they knew not what; but as the flag had been insulted and the majesty of the United States defied, that was enough for them. Twenty-two dollars bounty and fifteen dollars a month was no inducement and little thought of. Even as the raw levies flocked to Washington's camp after Bunker Hill, so these fresher levies were coming from forest and forge to support Abraham Lincoln, who now, thirty years after, seems almost deified to us in his simple greatness. It is hard to imagine our forefathers of the Revolution as other than men gray and grave in homespun garb of the Continental cut; but they were boys like these, ruddy and of cheerful countenance, like these, moved by a divine afflatus to fight for freedom. Then it was for the personal freedom of themselves and neighbors; but now, though few realized it, for the freedom of the down-trodden and the lowly. So God bless the boys that carried a musket then, and His poor should ever bless them.

In a few days the company officers were summoned to the Senate chamber to choose field officers by ballot. Adjutant General Hodgdon presided. He is still living, and all Maine soldiers remember him, imperious and energetic, yet kindly, and doing great work for the cause. We looked at each other askance, being hardly

acquainted as yet, and finally I proposed that
we put some regular officer in for colonel, as
none of us knew much about the business. This
was seconded, and some one had the name, taken
from an advertisement, of Edwin C. Mason, captain of the 17th Infantry, recruiting in Portland.
So we chose him colonel. Then it was suggested by a man from Kendall's Mills that
Selden Connor, about finishing his term of three
months' service in the 1st Vermont, and soon
coming home as sergeant, would know something about it, and would be a good man for
lieutenant-colonel, so we chose him. We made
no mistake there. Then they insisted on making me major in spite of my extreme youth, as
I was the only man in the regiment who could
drill a company. Even now I can recall the
thrill of joy and dread and gratified pride that
the unexpected vote gave me; but the responsibilities were too huge and I promptly declined,
and would probably have persisted in declining,
had not Mr. John B. Swanton and Colonel Harding, by their encouragement and insistence, almost forced me into it. I did not know then
that the principal duties of a major were to ride
on the flank of the rear division, say nothing,
look as well as possible, and long for promotion.
The two lieutenants soon heard of my unexpected exaltation, and promptly took the train

for their homes, neither being willing to take the captaincy; and it was only on my promising to be captain, too, till I could find a substitute, that I was able to get them back to camp.

It was intended that the 7th Maine should stay long enough in camp at Augusta to get some cohesion and be able to march together; but long before they did it happened that orders came to send us to the front. Imagine my consternation on receiving them, when I reflected that the colonel had not yet been allowed by the war department to accept, that the lieutenant-colonel had not come, and that I, the newly fledged major, had to take this mob of one thousand men to Washington. To make it worse, when the order to break camp came, it was a literal copy of the one used by Colonel O. O. Howard, a West Pointer, to take the 3d Maine out of Augusta. He had taken one used at West Point for some grand function by the corps of cadets, and it was longer than one of Grant's orders moving the army toward Richmond. I remember the tent pegs were to be pulled in order at tap of drum, and the operation of taking care of them would take a week to learn.

Now I supposed all this had got to be done, and I was appalled at my ignorance and inefficiency. However, my good friends, Colonel

Harding and Governor Washburn, cheered me up, and the task was accomplished during an entire summer night; but as I had not yet had time to get a uniform, and few of the regiment knew me, I think my personal interposition did not avail much. The gray of the morning found us in long line of battle, knapsacks packed, and fortunately for me it was not far to the cars; and when we got there the boys were anxious to get on, so it was with a happy heart that I felt the long train start, in spite of the fact that for me, as for others, mother and sisters were waving their handkerchiefs and looking their last at us through weeping eyes.

What man of all the vast host then drawing toward the Potomac suffered more or did more for the country than the widowed mother who sent her only son!

CHAPTER III.

" And lovely ladies greet our band
With kindliest welcoming."

BRYANT.

HANDKERCHIEFS waved from every farmhouse,
cheers arose at every station, while our band
played and the colors were flaunted from the car
platforms, and so we jolted on the most of the
day, the excitement not abating when in a
column, nearly a thousand strong, we filed into
Faneuil Hall to take a lunch provided by the
city of Boston. Many dignitaries watched our
noble appetites from the galleries, and when the
meal was disposed of all arose: long, lithe sons
of Aroostook, Indians from the Penobscot tribe,
pale-faced clerks from the towns, river-drivers
from the Androscoggin, sailors just off blue
waters, keen-eyed hunters from Moosehead Lake,
old soldiers of her Majesty, and a few of the
Irish who in all times have scented the battle
from afar, — all this mass of men, now so heter-
ogeneous, rose to their feet and made the welkin
ring with cheers for the Cradle of Liberty.

We took a boat that night, I think at Ston-
ington, and landed at Elizabethport, to find in

New Jersey and Pennsylvania the same exciting God-speed. When we came to Havre de Grace, orders reached us to stop in Baltimore, and many rumors came of fighting in the streets of the city. Who does not recollect the myriads of rumors that were always flying about in war-time? We had read as boys so lately of Rumor depicted as a bird with a hundred mouths and ears and an eye in each feather; and in those days there must have been many like it to have carried the stories that were always throwing in the shade the truth; and the truth required no exaggeration — it was sufficiently exciting in itself.

The 6th Massachusetts had fought their way through Baltimore, and it was thought that we would be obliged to do so likewise.

No ammunition had yet been issued to us, and on looking through the regiment I found that there was but one pistol in the command that had cartridges. So careful instructions were given to all to attack with the sabre bayonet any one who tried to molest us. We got to Rullman's beer garden in West Baltimore, however, without other greeting than sour looks, to meet a worse enemy. The place was surrounded by grog-shops, and in less time almost than it takes to tell it a goodly number of the 7th Maine were fast getting beyond control. As soon as possible I got over to Fort McHenry, and re-

ported to old General Dix commanding; and
after I had, with difficulty, made him compre-
hend that such a youth could be a field officer,
I procured a supply of handcuffs from him, and
before dark the unruly were safely confined
under an old band-stand; and the camp slept in
peace, except when occasionally awakened by the
sentinels, who, being without cartridges, would
shout out to each other to keep their courage up
during the watches of the night.

The next day was enlivened by a riot, as
many were discontented at the quality of the
soft bread furnished, and sought the quarter-
master to hang him, but that gentleman could
not be found, and after a time the riot was
quieted by bringing into use our single pistol,
and the firm front of the officers.

Soon many of the other troops came to see us
from camps not far away, and all remarked, as
we turned out for dress parade, the great size
of the sons of Maine. I remember, when any
one of the early Maine regiments passed, that
was the usual comment; but disease seemed to
revel in smiting the big men, and to particularly
select those who from their former occupations
should have been hardiest and most robust,
while none seemed to stand hardships better
than the clerks from the towns, the country
schoolmasters, and even those who had been

most delicately nurtured. Had any of us then had the slightest conception of the laws of health or known anything about taking care of men in camp and on the march, the record might have been different and the tall men on the right been more successfully preserved. Knowledge of this kind is more useful in war than that of tactics, and at any rate should be equally studied. One of the secrets of Napoleon's success is that he was a great master of this branch of his profession, and, while he might appear to be reckless of his men in battle, he was usually most watchful of their comfort and health in camp.

After a week in the beer garden, we were ordered to change to Patterson Park on the other side of the city, and in better discipline and form we marched the whole length of Baltimore, the band playing Yankee Doodle most of the way. Our camp here was an ideal one, and the surrounding people were mostly for the Union. Feeling was then intense on either side. The rebel ladies would get off the sidewalk if they saw a hated Yankee coming, but the loyal people entertained us to the utmost of their power, and the little children would take our hands and cling to us as we walked as far as the end of the block. Our band with Ingraham as leader was the old Bath Band, and night after night the young officers — and we were mostly

young — would go out with it to serenade the
fair, and in return receive the best of Maryland
good cheer, the best in the world, and there is
no better in America. Joe Berry, of the band,
would sing " The Sword of Bunker Hill " and
" Our Flag is There " as a finale, and when we
sauntered home by moonlight in the soft, flower-
scented Southern air, it seemed as if soldiering
was a very good business. Indeed, no one can
enjoy more than the soldier the respite which
sometimes comes in war. The excitement of
campaigning is delicious, the reaction from it is
not without its pleasure, and many of us were
already prescient enough of the future to feel
that —

> " Why should we be melancholy, boys,
> Whose business 't is to die ? "

CHAPTER IV.

WHILE in camp at Patterson Park Lieutenant-Colonel Selden Connor, since four years governor of Maine, returning from his three months' service, joined us. Colonel Mason was not given leave of absence from the regular army, so Governor Washburn appointed as colonel, Thomas H. Marshall of Belfast. He had been lieutenant-colonel of the 4th Maine, and was formerly a successful lawyer and president of the Maine Senate. Their arrival relieved me from anxiety and responsibility, and beyond teaching the line officers their bayonet exercise and the broadsword, and practicing fencing and pistol shooting, I had little to do but enjoy myself.

About that time I made the acquaintance of Dr. Washington, a surgeon in the army and a most fascinating gentleman. He claimed to be of the family of the father of his country. He had traveled extensively, had been entertained by the Sultan and the Shah, and seemed to have a smattering of every accomplishment — was a sort of "Admirable Crichton" — and why he attached himself to me I have never learned. He bought a horse for me and the horse turned out all right. He superintended choice dishes and loaded me with fine cigars. He introduced me to Thomas Winans, the great railway contractor, who told me of his Russian experiences and explained his cigar-shaped ship. He was a great friend of the lady abbess, and promised to present me to the "Secesh" society who were the "400" of Baltimore.

One day I went to call on him, but he was gone, and great search was made for him, but he was never found. He was a most accomplished and adroit rebel spy. I had to stand a good deal of chaffing about my friend Dr. Washington, but it may be that he wanted to be seen to be intimate with some Union officer, to avert suspicion. Two years later I heard of his death in battle at the head of a Confederate cavalry regiment in Kentucky.

We fared well in this camp, for a refined and skillful gentleman, unable to do full duty as a private on account of his eyes, took charge of our cuisine. Though our bill of fare was limited I can never forget Dr. Forbes's breakfasts of peaches and cream, followed by steak and fried potatoes, which he used to accompany by a

choice répertoire of songs and the guitar. I
think we were always hungry in those days, and
it grew upon us in the after campaigning until the engrossing subject was, where were we
to get and how were we to get something to eat.
It took precedence of our interest in the enemy.
Almost anything tasted good, and it was often
well that it was so. But we knew not how to be
thankful for the keen, unspoiled appetite of
youth, sharpened by the open air and constant
exercise, and as we were seldom confident about
the next meal we usually paid devoted attention
to the one in hand.

It was a custom, sanctioned by ancient military usage, for a major to have a servant, and I
had one; but I had not learned in Bowdoin College what to do with him, so, after dressing him
up in a sort of livery, I set to work to spoil him
and succeeded very well for a time. Fortunately
for him, however, he soon grew big enough to
enlist, and at sixteen years of age Sam was as
brave as Julius Cæsar. A regiment of such little fellows, like the "gamins" of Paris, would
have gone anywhere.

Our chief worry now was that the Army of
the Potomac, slowly organizing in front of
Washington, should move on the enemy and
leave us behind. This illustrates the happy
condition of benighted ignorance we were in. I

succeeded in getting permission to go to Washington, and with awe beheld the dome of the Capitol for the first time. Those who only know the city as it is now, beautiful among all the cities of the earth, could not realize the shambling, straggling, dirty, and forlorn place it was then. Most of the present public buildings were there then as now, but the spirit of the old South and of slavery had given it such a disheveled, shabby, tumble-down appearance, it hardly seemed worth fighting for. Army wagons and batteries constantly passing had cut up the streets, staff officers and orderlies were splashing through the mud, and the hum of warlike preparation was everywhere. I reported to General Howard, and volunteered to serve on his staff should a forward movement leave the regiment behind, and then went to the Treasury to get paid off, receiving $500 in gold. I felt much like Crœsus and the Count of Monte Cristo rolled into one, and I doubt if A. T. Stewart ever had such a poignant realization of wealth. The heavy twenty-dollar pieces soon got burdensome, and I took them back and exchanged them for greenbacks at par. Not very long after this same gold was worth twice as much in greenbacks, and it was practically the same as cutting down the pay of the army by half. There was very little growling about it, which shows what weight the names of things have with men generally. We were then having worse things to growl at, however.

During the balance of my visit my friend and townsman E. B. Nealley (lately mayor of Bangor), who was in the Navy Department, where he did many kindnesses for Bath boys, showed me the sights of the city, and dispelled the idea I had that the Army of the Potomac might move before spring. So I returned to camp in a more contented frame of mind, and was soon busy with a detail of men building a permanent fort at Canton, a suburb of Baltimore. Colonel Marshall, who had worked faithfully and incessantly in getting his command into shape, became very ill, and while he was lying between life and death the longed-for orders to join the army came. At daybreak of a winter morning we broke camp, and just as we were passing, with no drums beating, the house where he lay, his spirit took its flight. We believed then that rare distinction had been his could he have been spared. No old soldier but honors those so fortunate to be killed in battle, but the greater number of those dying before the battle should have their equal meed of honor. It is not such a difficult thing to do well in the excitement of action. An American in good health rarely does otherwise.

On reaching Washington, we marched down Pennsylvania Avenue to the White House and then through open fields and many camps, till we bivouacked for the night on Kalorama Hill, where the rain seemed to pour faster than anywhere else. This was scarcely a stone's throw from where the millionaire widow, Mrs. Patten, has lately built one of the finest houses in Washington. This camp was so dreary that some of us thought that we should prefer Willard's Hotel, and we got there wet through and through. It looked then about as now, only it was so full they were putting as many cots into a room as it would hold. I was fortunate enough to find my uncle there, and he caused the fatted calf to be killed for us; and the rain still coming down in sheets we accepted cots in a back corridor and were lucky to get them. Everybody there seemed to be *wanting* something: whether it was a contract or office or promotion or news or a drink, the feeling pervaded the atmosphere and was very infectious. Our stay at Kalorama was short. With joyful hearts we soon crossed Chain Bridge into Virginia at the route step, the band playing " Away Down South to the Land of Cotton ; " and we rejoiced, not realizing how many of us would never return to Northern soil.

CHAPTER V.

"And when our rights were threatened, the cry rose near and
far,
Hurrah for the bonnie blue flag, that bears the single star!"

WE went into permanent camp a few miles
south of the Potomac and became a part of the
Third Brigade of "Baldy" Smith's Second Division, Sixth Corps, to which we belonged all
through the war. Camp Griffin was the name
given to our part of the line, and the enemy
were supposed to be in front in mythical numbers. It soon fell to my lot to command the
brigade picket line. I had read as a child
"Hoyt's Military Instruction," which belonged
to my father when an officer in the war of 1812.
I remembered the rules for the defense of detached posts, so established my reserve at the
best house behind the line and caused it to be
pierced for musketry and had rifle pits dug to
command the approaches — which improved the
garden about as much as the embrasures did the
parlor walls. This did not please the owners,
two vinegary looking dames whose son and husband were riding with Ashby, but as I was
momentarily expecting the rebels to appear I

took great pleasure in my fortification. I don't think they appeared once that winter, however, though picket duty became very disagreeable as the novelty wore off and the frost and snow increased. We then thought it necessary for all to keep awake all night, and the advanced posts were visited very often. This most important duty was well learned that winter. Once the detail for picket duty was entirely of Germans, and the whole three hundred, marching homeward over the snow, as the sun was about to rise and the eastern sky had taken on a rosy hue, struck up in perfect harmony " Morgen Roth," — the red morning, a German war song, — and we thought of the warriors who ages ago sang the song of Roland before engaging in battle.

While on picket I shot with my revolver the only Virginians, I am glad to say, I killed during the war, and we cooked them in the camp kettle and found opossum fairly good. As we got more used to the country we would occasionally get a meal at some of the houses away from the line and pay them well and be as polite as possible, but though we longed for the society of ladies we did not get much nearer to it than to hear " The Bonnie Blue Flag " played on the piano in the neighboring room. It took some time to realize the enmity of the Southern women. We were always courteous and considerate to them and could not at first understand their universal bitterness, and that it was wholly patriotism in their eyes.

These changes in our mode of life and unwonted exposure made much sickness in the regiment, and scarcely a day passed that did not add to the growing cemetery over the hill; and the " Dead March in Saul," played by the band at each funeral, almost lost its sadness by repetition.

Colonel Mason finally secured permission from the war department to take command of us, and as he was a most excellent drill officer and disciplinarian we soon became proud of our proficiency. It was a sad bore for me to follow with the rear division during many hours of battalion drill, but the education was salutary. We had white gloves, shoulder scales, and new uniforms, and fancied ourselves very much like regulars. Many droll characters appear among a lot of men brought from so many places and avocations. Our regimental tailor, Dennis Mahoney, who was born near the groves of Blarney, and who claimed to be a relative of Father Prout, early became as well known as any. I first remember seeing him one frosty morning near the guard house, with feet fettered and a barrel put over him, above which his eyes were

twinkling. "Me bould Major, a man is a
man if he is in a bar'l," was his salutation, and
I had him set free at once. That evening,
while we were in the colonel's tent, somebody
scratched for admission and Dennis's head appeared very much the worse for wear. "Me
gallant Colonel," said he with a Chesterfieldian
bow, — "Sergeant of the guard, arrest this
man," shouted the colonel. "Ye poor little
grasshopper — to h—ll wid ye!" said Dennis
with immense disdain; and this took the colonel
in a tender place, for he weighed little over a
hundred pounds. Dennis had to go to the guard
house once more and sleep off his exultation and
dream he was again by the pleasant waters of
the river Lee.

A countryman of Dennis, one Thomas Mc-
Nillis, of Company D, his ramrod in his loaded
gun barrel and himself well charged with fire
water, started one day with the expressed intention of cleaning out the "buck tails," a
Pennsylvania regiment so called because they
wore buck tails in their hats, and who were en-
camped not far from us. He succeeded in
reaching a hill that commanded their camp, and
opened fire. They were aroused by Tom's ramrod swishing through their tents. He could not
load again, but charged the camp with the bayonet, and was soon so soundly thrashed that he
died not long after.

One night came my first independent command, and I received it with great joy. I was ordered to take two companies and go out some seven miles beyond our lines to intercept some of the enemy, who were said to be on the return from an expedition beyond our right. We started after dark and arrived at our destination by midnight; and I put my men carefully in ambush, after a method I had read was used by Marion and Sumter to confound the British. Breathless and breakfastless we awaited the coming of the foe. I intended to suffer them to pass our first ambush, which was to take them in the rear when our firing began, and each man had careful personal instructions; but, alas! they came not, and I don't believe there was a rebel within ten miles. It was lucky for them, and for us, too, perhaps, that they did not come; so we got back to camp again, and my brief dream of glory was sadly dispelled. We found the whole division wildly cheering for Grant's victory at Fort Donelson.

CHAPTER VI.

"When first under fire and you 're wishful to duck,
    Don't look or take heed at the man that is struck,
    Be thankful you 're living and trust to your luck,
    And march to your front like a soldier."
                                    Barrack-Room Ballads.

THE Army of the Potomac was now a well
disciplined and drilled body of more than a
hundred thousand men, and in better heart to do
fighting than it ever was in later years. During its first engagements all were anxious to get
into the fray, even officers' servants, and other
detailed men, taking their guns and their places
in the ranks of their own free will. McClellan
had employed all his matchless talents for organization during many months upon this army,
and near spring a grand review was ordered.
We hardly knew what we were marching out of
camp for, and some thought it was toward
Manassas and the enemy; but when we reached
our allotted position in line the sight was magnificent, indeed. More than one hundred and
fifty regiments of infantry in close column by
division, with cavalry and artillery in proportion, made a military spectacle never witnessed

on this continent, and rarely on any other. The regiments were full in numbers, the clothing and accoutrements new, and the foreign officers present, of whom a score glittering with decorations ornamented McClellan's staff, must have been impressed with the power and glory of the Republic. It took hours for the whole column to pass the reviewing stand, but in time we got back to camp, tired, thirsty, and hungry, though somewhat in excitement still, for we considered the review the presage of an early campaign.

The clamor of "On to Richmond" filled the Northern papers, and as they had no experience of Virginia mud it did not surprise us.

About the eleventh of March, we broke up our winter quarters, marched toward the enemy at Manassas, and spent the night in bivouac, — our first experience. I quote from a letter written at the time : "We have no baggage with us but our blankets. I enjoy this kind of life immensely. We expect to be in Richmond in a fortnight." We got there in a little over four years, but our hopefulness was pleasant just the same. Finding the enemy had evacuated Manassas, we turned toward Alexandria, making a twenty-mile march, which was a big one for new and untried troops, especially as it rained all the way. We had to sleep in the rain, without shelter, that night for the first time, and old soldiers will all remember the experience of waking up stiff and sore so often in the night and getting warm by the fire, and lying down to try it once more. To this day I cannot smell a fire in the woods without being taken back in imagination to Virginia again.

We camped some days near Alexandria waiting our time to embark for the Peninsula, drilling as much as possible by day and studying by candle light evenings. At that time I copied all the drawings in Mahan's "Field Fortification," and almost learned the book by heart, which I found very useful afterward, for there is a right way to dig even a rifle pit.

We embarked, March 23, on the steamer Long Branch for Fortress Monroe. That night Nickerson sang in his clear tenor "The Yellow Girl Dressed in Blue," Dr. Forbes, "The Cottage by the Sea" and other choice ditties, and Channing was as full of humor and mimicry as he was afterward in many harder places; and it waxed late before we sought our hard couches. The next morning we were steaming through the great fleet of transports gathered at Old Point Comfort, gazing with excited interest on the already historic Monitor. Our arms were soon stacked on the beach, and while many were tumbling in the sad sea waves some of us made a reconnoissance of the Hygeia Hotel; which was not the vast and stately pile now frequented by hundreds of guests, but a low and squalid hostelry that could offer no refreshment for man or beast. The poorest sutler's store in the Grand Army had better fare.

That night the dome of the Chesapeake Female College shone in the moonlight some three miles away. Certain associations made it a kind of shrine for me, as it had sheltered the previous winter one who has brightened my life for more than twenty-five years. So, after a smart gallop through the recently destroyed village of Hampton, out into what seemed to be the enemy's country, I came to the then deserted college, which is now the National Soldiers' Home. The young ladies had evidently left in haste, for many of their belongings were scattered about. The waters of the bay were glittering; off toward the enemy all looked misty, dark, and uncertain; home seemed very far away, and the realization of the seriousness of war would obtrude itself, though the charm of the night soon brought content after sadness.

> " Let fate do her worst, there are relics of joy,
>   Bright dreams of the past, which she cannot destroy."

Our brigade was soon sent on to Newport News and then forward again, till we were in the extreme advance, and I had the picket the first night. As the enemy was said to be immediately in front in great numbers, I fortified a house and put a strong guard on the main road. In those days the enemy were always said to be in front in great force, and unfortunately headquarters were always believing it as well as we subordinates. If we could have had such a secret service as Sheridan afterward organized, there would have been no siege of Yorktown.

About midnight, while I was over toward the right of the line, a sharp musketry fire broke out on the road and lasted some minutes till I got there, when the men reported that the enemy were advancing up the road upon them. As I had not noticed any flashes from that side, I went down the road and discovered an old horse and two cows killed in action. The cows were soon broiling on the fire of the picket reserve, and the regiment whose men did the killing were chaffed for many days. These men were zealous and even enthusiastic, but they were nervous and untried. Not long after, they and their opponents made, I believe, the best pickets and skirmishers too, the armies of the world have ever furnished, because they were not only brave, but so many of them were highly intelligent.

All I have written heretofore has been of playing at war, but the real business was now about to begin. We stayed in camp on the James River a few days, and I remember seeing some of our Maine hunters shoot birds on the wing with a single rifle ball, little thinking how the same men would soon be bringing down human game.

The advance to Yorktown in two columns began; Keyes on the left, Porter on the right, and the 7th Maine as skirmishers in front of the left column, and as we met the enemy first we had the first fighting of the campaign. The view of a major of infantry is exceedingly limited, and I can only pretend to give that view. I had charge of five companies on the left of the road. Our first march was to Young's Mills, where we found camps of several thousand men recently deserted, but no life. The next day, however, after guiding my four hundred skirmishers fortunately for six or eight miles through a woody country, Ayres's battery following close behind, we issued from the woods and swamps and came upon some of the rebels — our first rebels — a few cavalry and infantry commanded by an officer on a white horse, who immediately fired his revolver at us, and then all disappearing like the " shifting phantasmagoria of a dream." Pushing on in great glee because my line was so straight, after passing through another belt of woods, we saw Warwick Creek with forts beyond and enough of the enemy. The bullets were flying thick, but we did not quite realize what they were, and the order came to halt and lie down. Now our brigade commander had a scheme of his own to communicate with a picket or a skirmish line, which was to have a string of men extending back, shouting distance apart, to pass orders out to the line by shouting them from one to the other. An order came over this novel telegraph line: " Tell Major Hyde to go out and draw the enemy's fire." I did not like this much, but I had to go, so taking a few men we crept out through a fringe of bushes to the overhanging bank of the creek, where I climbed down to the water, and, everything looking sheltered and peaceful, I was trying to see if the stream was fordable, when a crowd of men appeared on the other side looking at me and I at them, both sides rather astonished. I suddenly remembered that I ought not to be there and plunged into the bushes, and fortunately ran the right way, as none of their shots reached me. It afterwards turned out that the general had sent an order " to cease firing," or something like it,

which was mangled in transmission. So after he
learned it he never used that telegraph line
again. Well, I had seen the foe face to face,
near enough to count his buttons, and I had
seen enough to satisfy my youthful intelligence
that there were not many people over there,
and that our skirmish line could take it as well
as not. So I begged for permission to advance,
but it was not allowed. Had we all known that
the place was Lee's Mills and the key of the
Yorktown line, we should have been tempted to
go over any way and save the weary days of the
siege of Yorktown.

I saw my first man killed that day — a shell
cut him in two. I think he was the first man
killed in the Army of the Potomac, Joe Pepper,
of Bath. He used to work for us at home, and
when I went out to help bury him that night and
took his wife's picture from his bloody pocket,
for a moment I would have given all I had in
the world to get out of the army ; the horror of
it was so cruel.

CHAPTER VII.

"Well, heaven forgive him; and forgive us all!
 Some rise by sin, and some by virtue fall:
 Some run from brakes of vice, and answer none;
 And some condemned for a fault alone."

Measure for Measure.

WE had been under fire for a dozen hours.
We were green troops no more and we fancied
ourselves veterans. Our pride disdained the wet,
the chilliness, the mud, all the detriments of Virginia. We were soldiers now. We had had our
baptism of fire and we had borne it well, at least
we thought so, and pride in our glorious profession swelled our hearts and made even the slow
falling rain and the sodden ground seem to sing
and to resound with our elation. They brought
up hard-tack, it tasted sweet; the cold coffee in
large tins seemed nectar, and the only drawback
was that we had neither pen nor paper to chronicle our doings for the people at home. They
were the chorus to this bloody drama. "What
will they say at home?" was to us as "What will
they say in England?" to Wellington's battalions lying behind the wheat-clad slopes of Waterloo. To deserve well of one's country is what

the soldier pines for, and it sweetens his sorry lot.

We were drawn back a little that stormy night and lay where we could in the mud and wet; but our hearts were warm, or we might have perished as the storm increased. The heavens seemed to open and the Virginia rain came down in sheets upon us not yet accustomed to its fury.

In the morning shells began gently dropping among us, and made a dull day gently exciting. We learned their weird whistle, a sound we became better educated to on many fields from Gettysburg to the Appomattox, but I do not think it became pleasanter as months rolled on. However, we could soon distinguish the dangerous shot from the ordinary, and the futility of dodging became more apparent. At last we were put back into a camp that was almost Venetian from its water courses, and I was sent with a Maine detail to cut and corduroy a road to the rear. In about a day we cut nearly a mile through the primeval forest, sending drives of fifty trees down at once, men of all States gathering in wonder to see it done; but these were the hardy lumbermen from Northern Maine who made a pastime of felling trees even like Gladstone.

The next day whistling bullets through our

camp sent us to the front to see a handsome repulse of the enemy by Captain George Morse,
commanding our picket. On their attack, the
outlying picket ran in, and Morse promptly ordered the reserve to charge. The consequence
was dispersion of the attack, a prisoner or two,
and rejoicing on our side, tempered with sadness;
for my friend George O. McLellan had fallen
with a mortal wound, but from where he lay
wounded he sent shot after shot from his rifle
into the flying enemy. He was only a sergeant
in the 7th Maine, but to the end of the war I
thought that a proud position.

One day I was ordered with three companies
to feel the enemy in front and ascertain his line.
We pushed out through the beautiful woods for
a while and they seemed as peaceful as a beautiful dream; but suddenly a man in front of me
jumped and fell prostrate, and the sound of the
ball striking him was like a sledge on wood.
But " Forward, boys, it is safer there ! " and soon
we came out in front of their works, and their
cannon belched out over where we hugged the
ground closely, while I made a hurried sketch
of the line. On my return, I reported to Major-
General Sumner, commanding the left wing of
the army, and gave him my drawing. The bluff
and gray old officer looked at me and seemed to
look me through and through, but my blue over-

coat gave no signs of rank. "You a major!"
said he. "My God! sir, you will command the
armies of the United States at my age, sir." It
always puzzled the old regulars to see us juveniles
playing soldier, as it may have seemed to them.
Night after night of picket, night after night of
sore trial, seems now the epitome of the siege of
Yorktown. Once we rode over to the right to
see the grandeur of the siege that McClellan was
modeling on that of Sevastopol. And he was
doing it in great shape, unaware that if he would
tell us on the left to go ahead we could soon
flank the rebels out of their holes.

It always seemed to me that McClellan, though
no commander ever had the love of his soldiers
more or tried more to spare their lives, never
realized the metal that was in his Grand Army
of the Potomac. We were never "put in" except in detail, and no troops before or since, I
believe, would better have justified "putting
in." He was troubling his patriotic and gallant
heart about the troops that had been taken from
him, and never appreciated until too late what
manner of people he had with him; no better
than other people, perhaps, but ignorant of danger, zealous for our cause, with health yet un-
touched by the miasma of the Chickahominy.
Not long afterward, twenty thousand of these
troops, under Porter, stood off Hill, Longstreet,

and Jackson, with sixty thousand men, from noon till the going down of the sun. And what might they not have accomplished on a direct assault! We would not have enjoyed assaulting the works at Yorktown proper, but on a twenty-mile line there were lots of other places to put us in.

But McClellan after all was in some sense an exponent of his army. We thought he did all things well, and so did he. How Magruder and Johnston and the rest must have chuckled at our slow movements, but if any one had hinted to us we were slow it would have been "pistols and coffee" at once. Still the grand man of the age was fretting his heart out at Washington over our barren bulletins of victory, and divining with his marvelous common sense how things were with us, even while his blind advisers caused him to take away division after division of the men we needed. We would have needed them even more had the muster rolls of the Confederates equaled the reports of McClellan's scouts. These reports were the principal cause of the failure of as pure a man and as popular a soldier as the century had seen.

CHAPTER VIII.

"Now's the day and now's the hour,
See the front o' battle lour."

BURNS.

WHILE we had been waiting orders to form
columns of assault, and recalling all the thrilling
stories we had read of forlorn hopes from Charles
O'Malley in the breach at Ciudad Rodrigo to
the storming of Molino del Rey, the day passed
on with little change in our surroundings. We
heard sometimes heavy guns on the right. We
saw the swamps become a little less flooded, and
at times it did not rain. Late one night our
orders came and little sleep followed them, but
in the early morning there was an unwonted
stillness as the long regiments filed out of camp,
and very soon we were told that the enemy had
departed. As we wended our way through their
deserted camps, there was an occasional explosion. We were warned to look out for torpedoes,
and we soon passed some deftly planted for our
undoing, and it seemed an unkindness on the
part of our misguided fellow-countrymen. We
had not had the time to get up much of a feeling of hostility to them as yet. We pushed

on in pursuit over fairly good roads, and were considerably delayed by Sumner's column crossing our path. Distant firing was heard at intervals in front from the cavalry and horse artillery, and crowds of contrabands passed to our rear, looking like so many old clothes-bags, but in great joy, as they believed the millennium had come.

We lay that night in a potato field, having soft but wet beds between the hills, and as it rained in the night they were softer and wetter by morning. About noon the next day, while Hooker's and Kearny's divisions were fighting in the woods in front, six regiments of us, under command of General Hancock, moved off to the right some miles till we were in sight of the York River, then turned toward the town of Williamsburg, and came to a milldam with a fort on the steep hill on the other side of it, which, fortunately for us, proved to be unoccupied. We pushed on across the dam, and, on gaining the hill, saw in front of us a chain of forts and the smoke of Hooker's fight in a direction that proved to the least experienced that we were moving straight on the enemy's left flank. As the ground became more open, and we got into line of battle, we could see how few we were, and the danger of being cut off appeared imminent, as the woods on our right were very dense.

Now, it is not my purpose to give other than my personal impressions, which are now dimmed by the lapse of thirty years, and I will not undertake to give a detailed description of the battle of Williamsburg. I was at first sent out with some skirmishers into the woods on our right, and I went beyond the men to see if there was any one there. The day was overcast, the woods were wild and tangled, and it was rather gruesome looking from tree to tree to see if a foe lurked behind. Coming back I was fired on by our own men, very properly, as I came from the wrong direction. Returning to the regiment which was lying down in line in open field, I could see in front the 5th Wisconsin and 6th Maine skirmishing with the rebels, and Wheeler's battery firing for all it was worth upon some redoubts, and soon from beyond Fort Magruder some three or four thousand of the enemy appeared. I did not then know that the general with his staff so clearly seen with them was Jubal A. Early, called the late Mr. Early at West Point, who once came so near taking Washington, who was afterward so unmercifully beaten in the Shenandoah Valley by Sheridan, and who is said to be still an unrepentant rebel. Our advance regiments fell back by General Hancock's order; on the Confederates came, and a fine picture of a charge they made. They were

at the double-quick, and were coming over a
ploughed field, diagonally across our front, to
attack the troops that were retiring. They
could not see us as we lay flat on the ground.
From my place on the left of the regiment, I
saw General Hancock galloping toward us, bare-
headed, alone, a magnificent figure; and with a
voice hoarse with shouting he gave us the order,
" Forward! charge ! " The papers had it that
he said, " Charge, gentlemen, charge," but he
was more emphatic than that : the air was blue
all around him. Well, up we started, and the
long line of sabre bayonets came down together
as if one man swayed them as we crossed the
crest, and with a roar of cheers the 7th Maine
dashed on. It was an ecstasy of excitement for
a moment; but the foe, breathless from their
long tug over the heavy ground, seemed to dis-
solve all at once into a quivering and disinte-
grating mass and to scatter in all directions.
Upon this we halted and opened fire, and the
view of it through the smoke was pitiful. They
were falling everywhere; white handkerchiefs
were held up in token of surrender ; no bullets
were coming our way except from a clump of a
few trees in front of our left. Here a group of
men, led by an officer whose horse had just fallen,
were trying to keep up the unequal fight, when
McK., the crack shot of Company D, ran for-

ward a little and sent a bullet crashing through his brain. This was Lieutenant-Colonel J. C. Bradburn of the 5th North Carolina, and at his fall all opposition ceased. We gathered in some three hundred prisoners before dark. Then the rain came, and though there is nothing specially remarkable about that, for it was always coming down, yet it made much difference with our comfort, and it is one of the trivial facts that will insist on being remembered.

I went over the field and tried to harden myself to the, sights of horror and agony. One gets accustomed to such things, just as doctors get accustomed to the dissecting table, but at this early day we were not much hardened. As it became dark we spread a lot of fence rails in the mud and sat on cracker boxes in our rubber blankets most of the night, for, between the excitement and the rain and the occasional shots of our picket just in front, we had no desire for sleep. Connor told stories and recited poetry, and we reiterated to each other our experiences of the battle with an enthusiasm that could not be quenched. Nor were the men much more sleepy. Beside their dim watch-fires murmurs of hushed conversation arose, and the phosphorescent glow on the faces of the dead in the fields beyond became more weird as the night sped on. Distant noises would have told older soldiers that the enemy was in retreat in the black darkness off toward Williamsburg, but we expected to attack Fort Magruder in the morning.

Our part of the battle was the beginning of Hancock's fame, and he always had a lively affection for the regiments who were in the " bayonet charge at Williamsburg."

The next day we did not move out of this rude bivouac. I went to see the doctors operate in a barn near by, and they had a pile of legs and arms that looked positively uncanny. We all wrote most exuberant letters home, and at night, while at dress parade, a great cavalcade was seen approaching, General McClellan at the head. He stopped before our colors, and in a graceful speech thanked us for the charge of the day before, which, he said, saved the day, and directed us to place " Williamsburg " upon our flag. We broke out into wild cheering, and no British regiments were ever prouder of the emblazonments of Talavera or Badajos than we, so recently from civil life, of the honors of our maiden field.

CHAPTER IX.

"Wut did God make us raytional creeturs fer,
But glory and gunpowder, plunder and blood."
Biglow Papers.

OUR marches were short and slow from Williamsburg to the vicinage of Richmond. Going through that ancient burgh where was the College of William and Mary, and where all the girls were patriotically clustering about the Confederate hospitals, we seemed a while in the world of Thackeray's Virginians, and almost expected to see the coach of Madame Esmond.

The next night the moon shone clear upon our picket lines, and upon the roofs of a stately mansion far in front. A spirit of adventure led Connor and me to slip through our guards and ride a few miles out into the rebel land, in the belief that if there, the enemy must be asleep. We rode up the long avenue of elms, up to the ancient and hospitable looking veranda, and, leaving our horses in charge of an orderly, began to explore the premises. Doors and windows were wide open. Half-packed trunks were lying about, and all tokens bore witness to the hurried flight of the family. We lighted can-

dles and explored the grand old rooms, looking
at ourselves in the ancient pier glasses, and
made acquaintance, in its sadness and desolation,
of a Virginia homestead of the olden time when
the county families vied with the nobility of the
England from whence they came. A trembling
black butler soon appeared and served us old
Madeira in quaint decanters. We sent his fel-
low-servants to act as sentinels and warn us of
the approach of the enemy, and made careful
exploration of the mansion. In the third story
a distinct snore became audible, and when we
had summoned its author, and fully expected to
bring in a rebel brigadier-general, we found we
had only waked a stray signal officer of ours who
had lost his way and put up there for the night.
As others less appreciative would, no doubt, have
taken the Madeira, we loaded up our steeds with
it and a memento or two. Mine was a feather
pillow, which luxury was soon after purloined
from me in turn. While we were looking over
the library of choice books, the darkies gave the
alarm, and we were at once in the saddle galloping across country toward the distant haze that
concealed our faithful pickets. Such little epi-
sodes sweetened the usual grind of campaigning
of which mud and hard-tack, rain and marching,
were the salient features.

As we drew nearer and nearer to Richmond,

one day we came to a crossing where four roads met. Above it was a weather-beaten and time-worn sign-board that no doubt was doing duty when Washington marched with Braddock; its legend read, with hand pointing westward, " 21 miles to Richmond; " beneath it another was nailed of the new pine of a bread-box, with a large hand pointing in the opposite direction, and " 647 miles to Gorham, Maine" showed unmistakably that some of our fellow-citizens had passed that way.

That night we camped in an immense wheat field at the White House on James River, the place where Washington was married. The plain was large enough for the bivouac of 75,000 men, and as the Army of the Potomac gathered in it with wagons and artillery the sight soon became grand. At this place a French officer whose acquaintance I had made came to call on me, but I was off somewhere, and he asked, " Vere is dat major, major — vat you call him? Somebody goes away, nobody can't find him; " and this closes my associations with the White House.

We pushed on one or two easy marches toward Richmond and the scene of our next fight, which I will suffer a letter written home at the time to describe:

" Day before yesterday we received orders for

detached service, and marched six miles on the Richmond road, passing General Stoneman's advance and crossing the Chickahominy Swamp after a short skirmish. We lay on our arms that night, and dawn showed us the village of Mechanicsville in the distance, where the rebels were posted in some force, and only four miles from Richmond. General Davidson pushed us forward on the left, and the rest of the brigade on the right of us followed by Wheeler's battery and a squadron of cavalry. The enemy let us get pretty near and then 'let fly.' Their first round shot struck in a ditch we were crossing, and the second seemed to knock Colonel Mason, horse and all, over. He lay in the bushes very pale, and faintly said, 'Take command, Major.' Connor was off on picket. We advanced till the general found a good position for the battery to open, and then he ordered us to halt and lie down. I put the regiment behind a ridge, and soon Colonel Connor came up and relieved me. The enemy bringing up more guns and the fire from the tops of the houses waxing hotter, General Davidson brought up two pieces of horse artillery, posted them himself well up to the enemy's battery, and threw us forward to support them. About this time I was thrown over by a cannon-ball which just grazed me, and when I picked myself up I saw how splendidly our fire was telling. The houses were riddled, chimneys knocked down, and the rebels were swarming from their places of concealment. They took themselves off so well that, when our line charged just after, our prizes of victory were only their knapsacks and many of their arms. The loss of the whole brigade was trifling, only about a dozen; ours, a few flesh wounds. Colonel Mason was insensible for some time, but is now all right. General McClellan rode up shortly after and pronounced it a 'dashing affair.' The forces opposed to us were said to be Howell Cobb's Georgia brigade and Dawes's Battery.

"It is somewhat remarkable that in every fight we have been engaged we have been drenched with rain.

"We left Mechanicsville that (last) night, and to-day move further to the left. We can here see the rebels quite plainly across the valley, and while at supper they threw a shot into us which did no harm. My tent is in a strawberry bed near a fine country residence, filled with wounded rebels. We had strawberries for supper, and the men have been luxuriating in green peas and beans, gooseberries, sweet potatoes, and 'hoe-cake.' I have had to take lots of quinine so far. I suppose people think one goes into a fight as the picture-books have it. I was blacked with smoke, my trousers were all caked with mud, my sword rusty, and I wet to the skin."

This movement to Mechanicsville on our right was made by McClellan, hoping to hear Mc-Dowell's guns coming straight down from Washington; but he never came.

I cannot remember a battle in which it did not either rain or rain just after, and we thought it was caused by " the red artillery."

CHAPTER X.

"The rebel vales, the rebel dales,
  With rebel trees surrounded;
The distant woods, the hills and floods,
  With rebel echoes sounded."

The Battle of the Kegs.

AND now I come to speak of the real fighting of the Peninsula. To my mind, nothing that came after exceeded it in the valor and tactical merit displayed or in reckless charges or losses in a given time. This feeling is emphasized as I read Union and Confederate reports. The splendid, full, and enthusiastic regiments of those days on both sides, the equality of numbers, unless the rebels were superior, made when the armies joined in battle a struggle as of giants. Their hearts were not then so eaten out by the fear of death long delayed. The best and the bravest who were to fall on so many fields were then with us. For *élan*, courage, hope, and pride in their cause, no armies before or since have surpassed the Grand Army of McClellan, and the Army of Northern Virginia.

After the skirmish at Mechanicsville we

camped near the Hogan House on the Chickahominy, and picketed that many-coursed swampy
stream. One day I had command of the division picket, and, after much fatigue in posting
them on hummocks and other dry points, I retired to the piazza of the Gaines House, which
overlooked the whole valley and was a fine point
of vantage.

Guards had been placed over the tobacco and
the turkeys, the icehouse and the hams of the
grizzly old rebel Gaines, who did not deign to
show his head to the Yankee vandals. As I
had nothing whatever to do but watch the birds
flying and listen to the grasshoppers, and as no
Lalage was present to draw even cold water
from the sacred stream near by, I ventured to
knock at the big front door, which was opened
by the grim Gaines aforesaid.

Putting on my best manner I requested the
loan of a book from his well-stocked library,
visible through the window, with which to be-
guile my loneliness. The old man soon returned
with a copy of the Patent Office Report of 1856
and handed it to me with simulated politeness.

The blow was a good one, but what could I
say? — the laugh was on me; but when the
picket at night was relieved, and each man had
on his back all the poultry and tobacco he could
carry, I am ashamed to say I looked the other

way, and I think then the laugh was on him. The negroes said that the week before Lee and Johnston had dined with the old gentleman, and we found he was a very big swell in Confederate circles.

The next time I went out there on picket, a yellow-haired lieutenant of cavalry came along and said he belonged to McClellan's staff, and wanted to explore the stream on our front. He asked me for some men to support him. I gave him a company under Lieutenant Nickerson, and soon the cracking of rifles through the green everglades told us anxious watchers that Custer was having his first skirmish.

From the Chickahominy to the Little Rosebud this daring soldier illustrated Anglo-Saxon courage, and when he lay with all his regiment around him in their eternal bivouac a chill struck to the hearts of every survivor of the Army of the Potomac.

The last time I saw him, a day or two before Appomattox, he was galloping to the front at the head of three thousand troopers, his yellow locks and red silk tie streaming in the wind, and a velvet jacket slashed with gold covered the gallant heart of the Murat of the Yankee cavalry.

Our part of Fair Oaks was to wait in column for hours for a faint chance to cross the bridges over the Chickahominy, to watch the cloud-burst of shells far on the other side, and to listen to the roars of musketry that sounded like the constant dashing of angry seas upon a rock-bound coast. The night before, I was again on picket, and about midnight found my advanced posts were knee deep in water. The stream was rising. I ran my horse to General Smith's headquarters, woke him, and told the tale. The division was to march at daybreak anyway, but out they came, and vainly tried the passage. The whole valley was inundated, trees were sweeping down with the flood, the frail bridges in our front were useless ; and so we missed taking a part at Fair Oaks, a most sanguinary and drawn battle. Sumner, farther to the left, had got over, for Sedgwick's iron nerve had pushed his division through all obstacles, and over better bridges, and hurled them in in time to save the fortunes of the day. Here the 3d Maine, with two full Bath companies, greatly distinguished themselves. General Howard lost his arm, and Adjutant-General Edwin Smith of Wiscasset, than whom no braver spirit was on the Peninsula, gave up his life among the plaudits of all Kearny's gallant division.

Inaction succeeded Fair Oaks, hot weather, poor food, poorer water, no vegetables, all hands in line an hour before daybreak, the ration of whiskey poured around in big tin pails, and quinine a necessity of life.

One day a regular officer, a friend of Colonel Mason, came to call. He was just from home, and if there was a " 400 " then, he probably belonged to it. We asked him to dinner, and to our horror the only dish, which was boiled rice, was burned. Of course we laughed, but it was really no laughing matter, for we were hungry; as indeed we were always.

Here I had my only illness during the war, and it came about in this wise. In an evil day, I gave five dollars for a jar of sutler's stuff all covered with yellow and green labels. I can see it now with a shudder. Soon after regaling myself and friends, I was traveling to the rear in an ambulance, my faithful Sam riding behind. He got me to bed somewhere near Savage Station in a field hospital, where my illness was pronounced an attack of chills and fever. After a few hours the cannon began to boom in the direction of our camp. I bore it a while, but could not stand it long; was helped on my horse, and before I got to camp again, where the cannonade of Golding's was going on, I was well, and in my right mind. Now this was not from any special anxiety to get into the fight, for I do not think we had that very much, but the longing to be with the other fellows came over one like a kind of fascination ; it resembled snake charming, when they were in it and we were not. I must say, however, that this desire weakened as the years went on. Though I was badly scared in every fight, I think it grew on me, and I was more scared in the last fight than in any other.

I heard a distinguished speaker say lately that he always dreaded going on the platform, and that Senator ———, one of our greatest orators, had told him he had never got over his fear of an audience. So it was in going into action ; but as in the speaker's case, after he became warmed up the feeling of fear passed away, so, with the soldier : if he was busy after he got in, his military stage fright soon left him.

CHAPTER XI.

"Once more unto the breach, dear friends, once more."
King Henry V.

OUR army was at this time straddling the Chickahominy; Porter's 5th corps, of twenty thousand men, was alone upon the right bank, and our (Smith's) division came next upon the other bank. Lee sent Stuart's Cavalry around our right, demonstrating that our weak point was there. Then he prepared to deliver the blow that at once established his reputation as a great soldier. Bringing Jackson from the valley, he ordered an attack with three of his great corps upon our exposed right, commanding in person himself.

All the afternoon (June 26, 1862) we heard heavy cannonading in the direction of our right and front, and as it grew dark could see the quick flashes of the guns, and later, in the increased quiet, the low surging sound of distant musketry. It would be hard to realize the anxiety one feels in listening to a fight one cannot engage in. We knew that McCall was at them, but with what result? At length an

orderly came dashing along with the glad intelligence that we had whipped the enemy commanded by Lee in person. Wild cheering broke
forth; our bands performed for the first time
since Williamsburg. That night a redoubt was
built on our picket line and a skirt of woods
cut down which unveiled our camps to the guns
of the rebels. At dawn the firing opened fiercely,
but more to our right. Could the enemy have
beaten us? We saw fires and heard heavy
explosions in the direction of Porter's camps,
and soon column after column appeared on the
flats across the Chickahominy above us, and our
glasses soon recognized the dirty gray uniforms.
Now our brigade was ordered to form on the
picket line, and they soon opened on us with
several batteries. We lay as flat as possible,
and could see Ayres bring up the division artillery and spiritedly reply. Then a Connecticut
battery of heavy guns opened, and after an
hour's firing the rebel batteries were silenced.
In the intervals of our own deafening fire we
could hear the cannonading going on with un-
intermitted fury on our right, and still the
heavy gray columns were pouring in upon
Porter. We all felt that we ought to attack
to make a diversion, though we did not know
that the 5th corps alone were still gallantly
standing off the assault of sixty thousand men ;

and they did it all that day until nearly sundown. The other division of our corps (Slocum's) was sent to Porter's assistance toward night, and we were relieved and ordered to follow Slocum. As our brigade line was forming, the enemy, seeing a movement of troops, opened suddenly with three batteries directly upon us. Our people came up firmly into line, but the New York 20th (German) went to pieces as the first shot struck among them just as if they were made of glass. We had difficulty in preventing them from breaking us as they swept off into the woods beyond. The air seemed filled with bursting shells. I saw two burst in the ranks of the 49th New York, piling the men in heaps, but the 49th closed up at once where they stood. I could not repress a thrill of exultation to see our line as steady as if on parade. This cannonade was the prelude to an infantry attack which succeeded, as it was intended, in preventing us from going to help Porter. Brooks and Hancock were in line in front, and we were ordered there to support Wheeler's battery. As we went I saw a long line of woolly heads burrowing as deep as possible in a ditch, and no one blamed our cooks and waiters much. Late that night the firing ceased. We all slept where we could on our arms, and the fight at Golding's was over, as

well as the great battle of Gaines's Mill, where
as good fighting against big odds was done by
our people as modern wars have seen.

The next morning it was discovered that the
enemy by the defeat of Porter had turned our
flank, and were in position to attack our right
and rear. Our guns were removed to the left,
our baggage train had already gone. The 7th
was sent with axes to the woods to make ob-
structions to delay pursuit. By noon this was
done, and the rebels opened fire from two directions. Our deserted camps were riddled, and
the scenes of the night before repeated. Soon
their infantry came forward. Our brigade had
the front this time, and, after an hour's fight,
our old antagonist at Lee's Mills and Mechanicsville, the Georgia brigade, was repulsed with
severe loss. I saw Colonel Lamar brought in
wounded and a prisoner. We called this the
"battle" of Garnett's Hill, and it had the effect of preventing any further attack that day.

We began to get uneasy by night. We
could not find anybody on our left, and we
knew there were none of our troops on the
right. We feared we were cut off, and as the
hours of the night went on we felt more sure of
it. It was an uncanny place, the stench of the
dead horses prevented sleep, water was scarce,
we could not even smile at Channing's jokes,

and the lieutenant-colonel's stories for once lost their interest. Two o'clock came: will our orders never come? Three o'clock: the growing day becomes dimly visible. Just as the light begins to steal among the trees, an aide dashed up, and away we go, hardly letting a canteen clink, and covering for a time the retreat of all the army. We called it then a "change of base," and as from the start there was hardly a day of the "seven days'" retreat in which we either could not have whipped, or did not whip, the enemy, it is proper enough to call it a change of base.

CHAPTER XII.

"I 'll shplit dem like Kartoffels;
I 'll slog 'em on de kop;
I 'll set the blackguards roonin
So they don't know ven to shtop."
HANS BREITMANN.

As we drew near the Trent House and passed on to Savage Station, fires and explosions were the order of the day. Here an immense pile of hard bread in boxes, enough to feed a province of starving Russians for days, was blazing; there a long line of whiskey barrels was being destroyed; farther on was a huge holocaust of hospital stores, and new clothing was at the will of every chance comer. The stragglers got drunk on the remnant of whiskey, and decked themselves out in new army raiment, but they were few in number. Generally the regiments were well closed up and in great spirits for a fight. On the immense plain beyond Savage Station several divisions were massed under General Sumner and held to attack the enemy supposed to be pursuing. Toward night, no one then appearing, the serried masses began to unravel themselves and stretch out on the road to the James River. Nearly all had gone but Smith's Division, when a sharp cracking of rifles where the Vermonters were stretched out in their always peerless skirmish line, announced that the hosts of rebellion were catching up with us.

In the gray of the evening the fight of Savage Station was made, and it was short, sharp, and decisive. The enemy were quickly rolled back into the woods from whence they came. Our brigade, in column by division, was advancing as support when they broke, and I heard, "Let's give them the bayonet!" repeatedly called out in the moving mass. As darkness fell we saw the lights of those helping the wounded mingle with the fireflies' glimmer in the fields in the direction of Richmond, while toward the James River bonfires showed us the road we were to tread that tedious night. Water was scarce and poor, and we patiently chewed twigs to assuage thirst, and plodded on through the dust. Sometime in the slow-moving hours I fell asleep, and my horse had his own sweet will till I was awakened in some other brigade by an alarm. Runaway horses were supposed to be the cavalry of the foe, and in an instant, as far as I could see, the road was as vacant as it was before we came there. The thousands of Yankees had taken to the woods, but not to flee away; they were on the alert, waiting for the horsemen who did not come.

At daybreak we crossed White Oak Swamp, and went into bivouac, everybody going to sleep where he halted. I was sent with two hundred men to picket the right, and I had scarcely got them into place when Stonewall Jackson, from the other side of the swamp, opened fire on the division as they lay, with thirty-six guns firing by battery. There was then "a mustering in hot haste." Mott's Battery happened to be in position, and was knocked into smithereens before it could open fire. General "Baldy" Smith was taking a bath in the only house in that vicinity, when a shell came through it, killed its owner, and away went division headquarters.

The regiments were ordered to form and march to the rear a mile, and from our position we were proud to see the 7th Maine, with Colonel Connor at the head, close up on its colors and slowly move to its allotted place over a plain storm-swept with shells. "Why don't they double-quick?" said we; but there seemed to be no hurry about the regiment that day. Then came the Germans (20th New York), and their large and fine array drew a perfect blizzard from Jackson's smoking guns. This was too much for the Dutchmen. They wore high, conical, black hats, and when they broke and ran the

plain was dotted far and wide with their hats
and knapsacks.

It is a tradition in our regiment that they are
running still, and their colonel, who, days before,
was talking about the blood he was going to
shed, and who certainly led the wild flight several
lengths, may not have stopped, for he was never
heard of afterwards.   There was later a rumor
that he was running a beer garden in Cincinnati,
but it was never authenticated.   Our experience
with the Germans, who were occasionally present
with us then, always made us somewhat skeptical
about their prowess later in the Franco-Prussian
war, but the trouble with them was that they
were badly officered.

Next came the magnificent Vermont brigade,
most worthy successors of Ethan Allen and the
Green Mountain boys.   Old General Brooks was
at their head, looking cross enough to stab some
one, one of his legs bandaged from a wound received at Savage Station.   They seemed to be in
no hurry either, and as parts of the regiments
would come to a standstill because those in front
were moving slowly, we could see the Vermonters
marking time to the screeches and wails of the
death-dealing rebel shells.   When they had
passed we seemed to be alone and deserted on
our low-lying woody hills to the right.

No orders came for us, and then we got into

shape to do what we could to resist the enemy's advance, but they only sent over some cavalry that a few shots drove back. We waited there several hours, and heard the fierce battle of Glendale raging over to the left; and finally I took the responsibility of retiring on the division, which was in a fine position a mile back, and found we were supposed to have been cut off. The results of this day were not flattering to the Confederacy, or especially so to us. The enemy had fiercely attacked a retreating army, and had accomplished nothing, while we had failed to strike back as we should have done because we were under orders to retreat to the James.

CHAPTER XIII.

"Serenely full, the epicure would say,
    Fate cannot harm me, I have dined to-day."
                                SYDNEY SMITH.

THE close of the conflict at White Oak Swamp brought us no rest, for after waiting till near midnight for a clear road behind us, we found ourselves again the rear guard, and filed out of the woods toward the James River. Ayres's battery was firing slowly in the direction of the enemy, and at each discharge lit up the gloomy forest; then gun after gun was limbered up and drawn away after us, and, as they passed our slow march, we saw the sturdy and gallant battery commander in the rear of all, stroking his black beard, and looking as handsome as he did on review.

Another long night of tramping, of dust, of thirst, of smothered objurgation, of weary struggle with sleep. "The night is long when comes the morn," but it at length found us near Malvern Hill, and gave us a few hours of desired repose. Then news came that the rebel army was fast approaching. The 6th corps was formed in two lines, one the "thin blue line," the other of regiments in column of division. Our verdict was that General Franklin had got us into fine form, as nearly the whole corps was visible, but hardly were we in shape when our beloved commander, General McClellan, at the head of a vast and brilliant cavalcade, approached us. He rode rapidly in front and saluted our colors as he went in the direction of the firing far to the left. We cheered him, for as yet to our feeble ken he had done all things well, and the love borne by soldiers to a favorite chief, if it does not surpass, is more unreasoning than the love of women. And so we waited and waited in formidable array and good position, and still the firing increased toward the left. We wanted them to come that day. Any excitement would have been better than the heat, the hunger, the thirst, and the yearning for some green food, for scarcely any of us had tasted even a potato for weeks. At a house behind our line were the headquarters of the division. In the kitchen near by, an ancient colored woman was found by Captain C., stirring a huge pot from which odors sweeter than those of " Araby the blest " were exhaled. The general and staff in the house were impatiently stalking up and down and eagerly waiting for their dinner. " Is it most ready, auntie ? " said our captain. " It 's mos' ready, honey," and as he began to taste it from a long iron spoon and to inquire kindly after her family, " Lord a massy, massa, be you the general?" said she. " Why, don't you know *me*, auntie?" said the captain, and in an instant was out of the hut with the big kettle; and when we saw him coming over the hill to us, little recking how the hot water was shaking and spilling over his legs, the soldier's instinct told us it was refreshment for the inner man.

The officers of the 7th bent the knee around the savory mess as if it had been an altar, and each putting his hand in the dish soon got his share of the bacon and the cabbage and the delicious Virginia beans. Our cravings for something green were so fierce, the fire of a battery or the thought of what the general might do could not have stayed us till the " platter " was as clean as that of Jack Sprat and his lamented spouse. Our late soup tureen was hardly hidden in a copse near by when staff officer after staff officer dashed up with sharp inquiry, but they could not have found a more innocent looking or ignorant lot of people, and our brave men on the line of battle who had had none of the toothsome compound were very considerate to us, for they did not even smile till the staff were searching some other brigade and the danger was over, when a laugh rippled from one end of the regiment to the other. " Who stole

GENERAL W. F. SMITH

the general's dinner?" was long a perplexing
query. I am sorry to admit we laid it upon the
Germans, and their fondness for loot made it
a credible tale. I had the pleasure two years
after of telling General Smith the bottom facts,
and he was able to laugh at it then, for it was an
after-dinner story.

As the day wore on, the firing toward the
left grew apace. After a refreshing bath in
a brook six inches deep, I conceived the idea
that it would be a good thing to see what was
going on, and soon found myself on Malvern
Hill, where I could admire the stern array of
what was left of the 5th corps, shattered, but
dauntless still, and wonder at the grand massing
of its batteries supported by the artillery reserve, and listen to the deafening roar of the
great guns from the war vessels far down on the
James. It did not seem that they would be
crazy enough to attack us there, and, fearing our
corps might be engaged before I could get
back, I did not stand upon the order of my
going, but returned at once. We lay in line till
dark, still listening to a most furious cannonade
and fusillade, which only ceased as the stars came
out, while in our front the cuckoo's song was un-
disturbed, until "the moping owl did to the moon
complain." We heard afterward how the best
chivalry of the South had for hours dashed

themselves upon Porter's lines in vain ; how Hunt's unsurpassed artillery had not allowed the enemy's attacking columns to keep their formation long enough to get near his guns ; how the army of Northern Virginia, than whom no better infantry ever fought in any field, were utterly broken and defeated ; and still we were to struggle back through the mud toward Harrison's Landing and the "fleshpots of Egypt." The order to go forward and seek our rations in Richmond would have been received with wild enthusiasm, for the rank and file of the Army of the Potomac were there for business then.

CHAPTER XIV.

"Who knows the inscrutable design?
 Blessed be He who took and gave!
 Why should your mother, Charles, not mine,
 Be weeping at her darling's grave?
 We bow to Heaven that willed it so,
 That darkly rules the fate of all,
 That sends the respite or the blow,
 That 's free to give or to recall."

THACKERAY.

IN a recent conversation with General Fitz John Porter, he told me that after the battle of Malvern Hill closed he sent an urgent message to General McClellan advising an advance on Richmond, but when it reached army headquarters orders had already been issued for retreat to Harrison's Landing and no attention was paid to his message.

The night after Malvern Hill was but a repetition of the other nights of the seven days' battles, except that rain set in. At first this made it more comfortable, but a Virginia rain is very piercing, and in time will get through rubber coats and blankets and trickle down into one's boots, and, besides, turn the sacred soil into the thickest red mud imaginable. And when this mud has been churned by the wheels of a wagon train twenty miles long, the result is almost incredible. We read that the "army swore terribly in Flanders;" so there was an ancient precedent for our teamsters.

In the morning the rain increased, and as we approached the rolling hills by the river I saw (and I expect unbelief) a mule go all under, except his ears, in the mud. He was not a very large mule, and he certainly was not a playful one after he was dragged out.

The river bottom at Harrison's Landing was large and easily defended. The gunboats looked after each flank, and the ground in front was open. It was the hottest place we had yet discovered, and there was a plague of flies, but we got on clean clothing and dressed our scurvy sores, and, when a bushel of young cabbages were procured from a transport ship, life seemed to be worth living again.

An officer in a marching regiment has but a very limited field of vision, so far as military operations are concerned, and I am trying to keep to my own field of vision only.

One night we were awakened by round shot shrieking by us from the rear, and a strange sensation it was. The rebels had posted a battery on the other side of the James, and for a brief time had the whole Army of the Potomac for a mark. The heat, the monotony, and our ill success, added to the malaria of the Chicka-hominy, produced a frightful amount of sick-ness. I think about half of our regiment were sent to the hospitals North, and, as usual, the most stalwart men were first attacked.

As there seemed to be no prospect of employ-ment, I succeeded in getting ten days' leave, and, tough and healthy, though reduced to one hundred and twenty pounds, I took ship for my far Northern home. How good the soft bread tasted; how strange the beds; how close the rooms; and the girls, how wildly beautiful. The holy emotions of a mother's welcome are beyond my feeble pen. The days flew by on angels' wings, and again the farewell and the long railway journey southward.

On arriving at Fortress Monroe, we found that the army was moving down the Peninsula, and the only way to find our regiment was to wait for its coming. A few of us went to the Atlan-tic House, Norfolk, for two or three days to have our last experience of luxurious living for some time, but at length the 6th corps appeared, and our comrades, lean, embrowned, and ragged, received us with laughing eyes. While in camp till embarkation, we used to send small negroes out for oysters, and cook them on the river bank as soon as brought in; and till then we had never really been acquainted with the Ameri-can oyster.

The lieutenant-colonel falling ill, I at last was in command of the regiment, and to say I was proud and happy with my lot is by far too inexpressive. Our time came to embark for Alexandria to join General Pope's army, supposed to be fighting near Washington, and while we were eager to do our duty, it was an unpleasing prospect to be placed under command of a general who had insulted the Army of the Potomac in his orders, and whom we already had sized up for a braggart. If McClellan and many of his generals shared this feeling they could hardly do otherwise, for it was almost universal with the rank and file.

We went into camp near Alexandria for a night, but before our horses and baggage had arrived, and without artillery, we were started out in support of Pope. I had then the experience of a twenty-mile march over the stony pike with new boots on, under the stimulus of the distant roar of cannon. Franklin was afterward accused of slowness and delay on that day, but footsore and weary I could have testified strongly to the contrary. We filed into a cornfield for the night's bivouac. Our mess cart had been left behind, but roasted ears of corn made a good supper, and the night was comfortable without blankets. Young regimental officers had not even then learned how to make themselves comfortable while campaigning, perhaps because we thought the hardships inevitable. We often fared worse than the men, and did not like to borrow from their sometimes scanty rations.

Early in the next day's march, we reached Centreville Heights and halted. The panorama was magnificent. Far in the distance, in open rolling country, a great battle was going on. The battle smoke stretched on both sides as far as the eye could reach, and its change of position only announced which side was winning. After some time it became painfully evident which side it was, as our line contracted toward us, and the hills and fields became dotted with the straggling and the wounded. I was ordered to throw the regiment out as skirmishers a mile to the left, lest the enemy might attempt to pierce between the retreat and Centreville. To take care of a few hundred skirmishers when dismounted and lame is not a sinecure, but we got there at last, and from the summit of a high stump I anxiously waited an attack till dark. Then in the usual rain we were withdrawn to a wet bivouac of an hour or two near a house on the hills of Centreville. While watching the battle I had been wondering where my dear friend and classmate Sam Fessenden (son of William Pitt Fessenden, our distinguished Senator) was, and how it went with him. He was, I knew, on Tower's staff in Pope's army, but my gloomy forebodings did not tell me that in the house so near he lay mortally wounded, brave and resigned to the last.

About eleven that night we were roused up and ordered to march back some miles toward Alexandria to form across the pike, and to stop all stragglers. It almost made me feel mutinous to drag out our tired men, but it was done in some way, and by morning we had over two thousand of Pope's army in a great corral.

Thus ended the second battle of Bull Run; a great disaster to our army. The only things I can now admire on our side, were the wise discretion of Porter in not attacking Jackson's right when so ordered, because Longstreet was between them, and the persistent fighting of the 1st corps under poor leadership.

CHAPTER XV.

"So thus did both these nobles die
Whose courage none can stain."

Chevy Chase.

For days after this battle of Manassas (as the rebels called it) affairs on our side seemed to be in a state of disastrous collapse. Before we left the heights of Centreville in a storm of thunder and rain, we saw shells bursting vigorously over the woods toward our right and rear, and crashes of musketry were sometimes audible in the turmoil of the storm.

At Chantilly, Philip Kearny, a paladin of old, though born in our times, and the soldierly first governor of Oregon, General I. I. Stevens, made this Virginia forest illustrious by their deaths. From the day he left his arm at the gates of Mexico, General Kearny had illumined a record, the pride of every American soldier. His gallant foes returned his body to our lines in sorrow. How we all honor the courage to do and dare, but when this is conspicuous among thousands, we can almost envy the death which illustrates it. General Stevens had a son who afterward became known to me, and he was one whom youth only prevented from rising to great heights in the military career. Some years later he was the first man to ascend Mount Rainier, and at the summit his party was saved from destruction by the volcanic heat still remaining in a mountain cave. The people of Tacoma when I visited there were still loath to believe that any one attempting it had ever come back from the summit alive, and the Indians had a tradition that one of their choice spirits of evil made there his dwelling-place and forever forbade human approach. Any who knew Hazard Stevens would not doubt his daring or his story.

What a gloomy time it was tramping back toward Washington! How the rumors of disaster on disaster came to dispirit us! But soon came the news that General McClellan was to the fore again, and every heart was lighter. Confidence seemed to cling about this man. Why was it? He proved no Napoleon, but we all believed in him. May not his innate purity and goodness have forced the homage we paid to the military genius we assumed for him?

As we approached Washington the stalwart new regiments of the second three hundred thousand call greeted us from the earthworks, in their clean new uniforms, but the Army of the Potomac looked very much like Falstaff's army then. How we cheered McClellan as we passed

his headquarters, nearly opposite where Worm-
ley's Hotel now stands.

Colonel the Baron Von Vegesack was in command of our brigade that night, and he was soon
to make his regiment, the runaway Germans,
the soldiers they were intended to be. Of all
the foreign officers I knew, and there were scores
of them with us, he was the best. None of the
old captains of Gustavus Adolphus did more
honor to the fatherland. He is now a major-
general in well-earned retirement in his native
Sweden, but he deserves thanks from the Republic in no less degree than Lafayette, only that our
needs were less. He has long passed the allotted
age of man, and I have no doubt that all the
honors he has received at home will fade as he
remembers our plaudits when he breasted the
storm of rebel bullets at Antietam and redeemed
the honor of the 20th New York Volunteers.

Orders were very strict that night that none
should leave the column which was pushing out
toward Tenallytown, but a very polite request
to Colonel V. got two or three of us an hour's
leave and a chance to mingle with the festive
throng at Willard's, and to see some friends
from home. A long midnight gallop brought
us back again to the sleepy throng just entering
Maryland, and enjoying their first taste of campaigning on Northern soil. Our next bivouac

seemed very conveniently situated as to chickens, and corn, and honey, and apple butter, and, like the Israelites of old, we looked upon the land, and it was good. The girls no longer made faces at us from the windows, and the people were down at their front gates with cool water, at least, if they had nothing better. It seemed like Paradise, this Maryland, and many were the blessed damosels we saw therein. Where was the man " who would not dare to fight for such a land?" But many of her best sons had become tainted with the heresy of secession, and were over yonder beyond the blue mountains waiting to give us the worst blizzard of cold lead we had yet encountered. I don't remember that we got very tired in these first marches after Lee. They could not have been very long ones. The regiments were quite small. I was still in command, and used to count mine once or twice a day, in the hope of finding a few more present, but we never had in this campaign more than two hundred and twenty-five. They were all seasoned veterans and equal to anything. I did not believe the same number of soldiers of the great Frederick could have stood against them. I was boyishly sanguine about what these people of the 7th Maine could do in the business they were engaged in, and, as I look back over so many years, I cannot but

COLONEL ERNST VON VEGESACK

acknowledge that they always justified my faith in them.

When camping in Baltimore, I had conceived the idea of learning by name every man in the regiment. As I had plenty of time, it was accomplished, and proved of vast use in many ways. I learned first the sergeants, then the corporals, then the tall men on the right of companies, and so on, and I earnestly commend the idea to any one who has occasion to command men. If you have the opportunity to do anything for a man, and there are plenty of such chances in war-time, he likes so much better to be known personally.

The farther we penetrated this favored land, the happier we became. Our past sufferings on the Chickahominy were but a dream, and we were a light-hearted army of some fifty or sixty thousand youthful soldiers when we drew near to the rugged crests of South Mountain, little recking whether the passage of its passes was to be disputed, or rough climbing only was to be our portion.

CHAPTER XVI.

"Oh, what is Death but parting breath,
    On many a bloody plain
    I've dared his face,
    And in this place,
    I'll meet him yet again."

BURNS.

AFTER several slow and deliberate marches, we drew near the South Mountain range, near Crampton's Gap. As our column got to the little town of Burksville, we could see Slocum's, our first division, in line and apparently about to force the passes, when the smoke of a battery on the far mountain side was soon followed by round shot shrieking overhead. We were ordered to take the double-quick, and through the street of Burksville we went, while cannon balls crashed among the houses, and the women, young and old, with great coolness, waved their handkerchiefs and flags at us. It was very refreshing to have the sympathy for once of the female part of the community. That and the clear mountain air made our campaigning such a contrast to the sickening surroundings of the Peninsula. Slocum's people went right up the pass, driving all before them, and we close after, in support, having all the excitement and exhilaration of a fight without its usual bloodshed. The mountains were echoing the rattle of a contest over to our right, where the 9th corps were forcing Turner's Pass, losing General Reno and many men. On the whole, this battle at Crampton's Gap was very creditable to our arms. We had three thousand men actually engaged, and the enemy two thousand; but ours had to climb up to them, which more than made up the difference. We got four flags and four hundred prisoners, and General Franklin could congratulate himself upon a successful encounter, — well planned and quickly over.

That night on picket at the summit of the range, I suffered from a bad toothache till morning dawned, when I rode in search of relief. After some miles, I came upon a country doctor's office. He was a very small man, and he tried to get that tooth out with a dental instrument of the last century, which was a sort of pry, — a small crow-bar. He was not strong enough, and after repeated efforts he summoned a passing teamster to his assistance, and the work was soon done.

That day we marched over into Pleasant Valley, where the faint boom of cannon from distant Harper's Ferry could be heard. The division was off by itself, and, as we could see a rebel line stretching across the valley a mile or so in advance, we expected a fight of our own. It appeared as if we were going to the relief of Harper's Ferry, but the distant firing suddenly stopped, which was sad evidence of its fall.

No advance was made, and at dawn, after a refreshing night in a half-filled hay-cart, I started off at the head of a high-spirited and happy regiment toward — we knew not what. But the angel of death was already hovering over the Antietam, and the Army of the Potomac was converging toward its bloodiest battle.

About nine o'clock the firing ahead of us became louder, and reminded us of Fair Oaks, and we soon were meeting hundreds of wounded coming to the rear. The 77th New York was just in front on the road, and I could not see much beyond them for dust; but as we passed acclivity after acclivity, and the diapason of the artillery and the rattle of small arms grew louder, we all felt we had got to brace ourselves, for the trying moment must soon come. The regiment looked so small, I made our eight or ten drummers and fifers arm themselves with guns picked up by the roadside, and join their companies. I could see occasionally men fall out from the regiments in front; but only one of ours, and he was sick, went to the

rear. It was refreshing to turn from the crowds
of wounded streaming back and look at the firm
set faces behind me, every one of them known to
me personally, and never known to lack nerve
in danger. But the 77th began to double-
quick as we came to some woods; we followed suit and soon passed by the 10th
Maine, that splendid regiment reduced to a
small squad. I asked for Beal and Fillebrown,
and was told they were down. Then I could
see the long line of Germans moving obliquely
to the left, while the 77th were going straight
on, when Captain Long, our adjutant general,
ordered me to go in on the left of the Germans.
It took but an instant to get the regiment forward into line, and then, left half wheeling like
a large company, we were out of the woods, and
the whole magnificent panorama of the field of
the Antietam was in full view. The Germans,
some eight hundred strong, were moving in fine
line, and looked so well that the whole fire of
the enemy was being concentrated upon them.
Colonel Vegesack and his field officers were
riding behind them, and pushing them on in the
most spirited manner. Seeing a body of the
enemy about some barns on our left flank, we
charged them, tearing the rail fences down as
we went. We soon drove them out, losing
a dozen men, and then dashed back again at the

run and lay down on the left of the Germans, who had lost heavily.

I remember in this charge passing over what had been a Confederate regiment of perhaps four hundred men. There they were, both ranks, file closers and officers, as they fell, for so few had been the survivors it seemed to me the whole regiment were lying there in death. Their clothing was of gray, or butternut color, and my impression was that they all had red or very light hair. At this time I saw Lieutenant Emery of Skowhegan jump in the air and fall rolling over several times apparently in great agony, but he was back with us in a short time: a bullet had struck his belt-plate.

It was now about one o'clock. We had re-taken the line we were ordered to retake. Five or six of our batteries were firing over our heads at as many of the enemy's batteries near the Dunker Church, which were busily returning the fire. The Irish brigade were charging up to the line over to the left; the Vermonters came up deliberately to our left and rear, and then we hugged the ground for several hours. Where we were, a lot of boulders in front protected us fairly well, but it was more open in front of the Germans, and every few minutes some of them would be struck and go to the rear, while scarcely any of our regiment were injured. I went over to Colonel Vegesack and told him they were specially singling him out, as his colors were held so high, and advised lowering them a little. " Let them wave : they are our glory," said the brave old Swede, and he kept on riding back and forth behind the regiment, revolver in hand to shoot the skulkers, the most prominent object in the field.

While on the Peninsula, a private named Knox, who was a wonderful shot, got permission to use his own rifle, a valuable weapon. As we lay under the storm of shot and shell, he asked me to let him go out in front, and every few minutes for an hour we heard his rifle crack. I found a place where I could see his work. He had driven away every one from a section of guns. As fast as a man would come forward to fire, Knox would tumble him over. A general officer and staff came into view, and his horse was promptly knocked over, and as promptly they all disappeared. At the end of an hour or so, he came in and disconsolately showed me his pet rifle. A piece of shell had struck the breech and completely ruined it ; but he took three rifles left by the wounded and went back to his deadly work.

From where we lay we could see Richardson's division beyond the Vermonters on our left, and in the far distance, the long-delayed efforts of Burnside and the sturdy lines of the Confederates opposing him, and they were almost perpendicular to ours ; off to our left and rear was Porter's corps, idle. But hills forbade all knowledge of what was being done to the right, and the smoke of many guns made it impossible to see to our rear, whether reinforcements were being brought up, or whether there were indications of our being ordered forward. It was drawing near five o'clock. Custom had brought indifference to the fire, and we were expecting soon to be relieved, little knowing that in a few minutes more the 7th Maine were to find their Balaklava.

CHAPTER XVII.

"Was there a man dismayed?
Not tho' the soldier knew
Some one had blundered."

TENNYSON.

COLONEL IRVIN of the 49th Pennsylvania commanded our brigade at Antietam. He was a
soldier of the Mexican War, and had been
wounded at Resaca de la Palma. He was a
gallant man, but drank too much, of which I was
then unaware.

Between four and five o'clock, a Maryland
battery was brought up on our line, and Upton,
Slocum's chief of artillery, came up to look
after it, and Colonel Irvin followed him. As
Colonel Irvin passed the battery, its commander,
who was Dutch, complained bitterly that sharpshooters were picking off his men, and pointed
out where they were, near some haystacks by
Piper's barns. These were not far from the
Hagerstown Pike, a short distance from the
main street of Sharpsburg, and behind the
centre of the rebel position. Colonel Irvin rode
to where I was lying on the ground, and said,
" Major Hyde, take your regiment and drive the

enemy away from those trees and buildings."
I saluted, and said, " Colonel, I have seen a
large force of rebels go in there, I should think
two brigades." What I had seen must have
been reinforcements going to repulse Burnside.
" Are you afraid to go, sir ? " said he, and repeated the order emphatically. " Give the
order so the regiment can hear it and we are
ready, sir," said I, which he did, and " Attention ! " brought every man to his feet. We had
two young boys carrying the marking guidons,
and I told them to go to the rear, but they pre-
tended to do so and afterwards came along.
One of them, Johnny Begg, soon after lost his
arm, and the other, George Williams, was
buried on the field. Color Corporal Harry
Campbell had the colors, and I started to give
them to Sergeant Perry Greenleaf, but Campbell felt so badly I let him keep them. I gave the
order to left face and forward, and we marched
over in front of the Vermonters, as the ground
immediately before us was too rough, and was
also more exposed to the batteries by Dunker
Church. Then, facing to the front, we crossed
the sunken road, which was so filled with the
dead and wounded of the enemy that my horse
had to step on them to get over. We stopped
in the trampled corn on the other side to
straighten our line, and then I gave the order to

charge, directing the regiment on a point to the right of Piper's barns. We were moving at the double-quick down into a cup-shaped valley, fifteen skirmishers under Lieutenant Butler in front, Adjutant Haskell on Colonel Connor's big white horse on the left, and I to the right on my Virginia thoroughbred. My feeling was first of great exhilaration, which was quickly dashed by that wretched Maryland battery, who, thinking to open over our heads, took four men out of my right company at their first shot. Seeing Haskell had fallen, and old "Whitey," too, I rode round in front of the regiment just in time to see a long line of rebels rise from behind the stone wall of the Hagerstown Pike, which was to our right and front, and pour a volley into us, which did not do so much damage as was to be expected, we were going so fast. At this, I gave the order, "Left oblique," bringing us behind a rise of ground which protected us some from the fire of the stone wall, and then forward to a hill just to the right of and beyond Piper's barns. As we breasted this hill, being some twenty feet in front of the regiment, I saw over its top before they did, and there were several times our number waiting for us at the "ready," so I gave the order to "Left flank" before any of my line appeared over the hill or came in sight of our opponents, and then directed the column, still at the double-quick, by Piper's barns, from which the rebels had gone, straight to a clump of trees where there was a fence and cow-yard, and on to the orchard beyond Piper's house, as I had seen a force running in that direction to head us off.   The men got through the fence easily, and, as Sergeant Benson was wrenching it apart to let my horse through, a shot struck his haversack, and we had to laugh at the flying hard-tack.   As we went up a rise of ground into the orchard, we came in sight of the Confederates who had been waiting for us beyond the hill, and they fired several volleys, and then charged after us.   Here we met our heaviest loss.   My horse was twice wounded, and as he was rearing and plunging I slipped off over his tail, and can remember, in the instant I was on the ground, how the twigs and branches of the apple-trees were being cut off by musket balls, and were dropping in a shower.   Finding he had only lost his back teeth, and had a charge of buck and ball in his hip, I mounted quickly.   I saw the regiment had got into line, and, while their numerous pursuers were coming through the fence we had passed, had given them a terrible fire, as the pile of dead found there after the battle attested.   Our survivors had no ammunition left.

While we were charging down the valley,

Harry Campbell, carrying the colors, was struck in the arm. He held it up to me all bloody, waving the flag. "Take the other hand, Harry," said I. When halfway through the orchard, I heard him call out as if in pain behind me, and went back to save the colors if possible. The apple-trees were short and I could not see much, but soon found the pursuing enemy were between me and the regiment, and I read "Manassas" on one of their flags, so I turned about and as quickly as possible gained the corner of the orchard and found the regiment had got through the tall picket fence. While uncertain how to get out, I was surrounded by a dozen or more rebels, but with a cry of "Rally, boys, to save the major," back surged the regiment, the muzzles of their Windsors were pushed between the pickets, and few of my would-be captors got away. Sergeant Hill with his sabre bayonet cut through the rails and I was soon extricated. Our batteries had been for some minutes throwing grape into the orchard, which aided us much, though we were more afraid of the grape than of the enemy. I then formed the regiment on the colors, sixty-five men and three officers, and slowly we marched back toward our place in line. The batteries by Dunker Church opened on us at first, but I guess they thought we had pounding enough, for they stopped after a few shots. But our main line rose up and waved their hats, and when we came in front of our dear comrades, the Vermonters, their cheers made the welkin ring. General Brooks had told their colonels when they begged to follow our charge, "You will never see that regiment again." In my judgment, we only needed the Vermonters behind us to have cut through to the river, and a few more brigades in support would have ended the business, as at that moment Lee's much-enduring army was fought out.

We did not take a large space on the line as we lay down in the falling darkness, and when Channing, Webber, Nickerson, and I got together under one blanket for the night, we were womanish enough to shed tears for our dead and crippled comrades. Fifteen officers and two hundred and twenty-five men in the morning, and this little party at night! We had the consolation of knowing that we had gone farther into the rebel lines than any Union regiment that day, that we had fought three or four times our numbers, and inflicted more damage than we received, but as the French officer at Balaklava said, "It is magnificent, but it is not war." When we knew our efforts were resultant from no plan or design at headquarters, but were from an inspiration of John Barleycorn in our brigade commander alone, I wished I had been old enough, or distinguished enough, to have dared to disobey orders.

REBEL REPORTS.

The following is from the report of George T. Anderson of the 11th Georgia regiment, and a brigade commander who commanded the force pursuing us : " I moved back to this position, which was approved by General Hill, who, riding forward to the crest of the hill in our front, called my attention to a line of the enemy advancing apparently to attack us. Suffering them to come near us, I ordered my command to charge them, which they did in splendid style and good order, killing and wounding many of the enemy, taking several prisoners, and routing the remainder. We could not pursue them as far as I wished because of the severe fire of artillery directed against us from long-range guns that we could not reach. In this charge, parts of Wilcox's, Featherstone's, and Prior's brigades participated with mine, and all officers and men behaved admirably."

From the report of Captain Boyce, Light Battery, South Carolina Volunteers : —

" About five P. M. a heavy fire of musketry began on my right and rear. I immediately ordered out my two pieces, crossed over to the slope of the hill lying in the direction of the town, and put my pieces in battery commanding the crest of the two hills to meet the enemy if he should compel our forces to retire. I then went forward and placed my guns on the hill within canister range of the enemy. A few shots soon drove them beyond reach of canister. I afterward used solid shot, cutting down his flag and driving him back."

From the report of General Rodes : —

" It is proper for me to mention here that this force with some slight additions was afterward led through the orchard against the enemy by General D. H. Hill, and did good service, the general himself handling a musket in the fight."

From the report of Captain Feltus, commanding 16th Mississippi regiment : —

" The enemy advanced upon us in line of battle about four or five o'clock in the afternoon. The remnant of the regiment in their proper position in the brigade moved forward and met the enemy in the orchard by the barn and drove them back."

These are fair samples of the reports of the other side. There can be no mistake about their referring to our fight, as it was the only fighting on the right or centre of the line after two o'clock that day. The reports also plainly indicate the number of people we were contending with.

Early in the morning General Franklin and General Smith relieved Irvin from command, and ordered us to headquarters as a guard. General McClellan came to see our colors, which had been brought off by Corporal Ring and were riddled with balls. I was told he said many kind things, but at the time I had gone out to the orchard to see if I could find any wounded. I found Harry Campbell, hardly cold, propped up against a tree with his pipe beside him. As they kept firing on me, I could make no arrangements to bring the bodies off that day. The wounded had either died from the night exposure, or had been taken by the rebels to Piper's barns. Many had got back during the fight to our hospitals.

We expected to renew the attack this day. Why we did not was a mystery then, but the real reason was in McClellan's over-estimate of Lee's numbers. He always saw double when he looked rebelward. That night we slept in the woods where we were first attacked. I saw two officers under a blanket, and turned in close beside them to be safe in one direction from being run over in the night. When morning dawned, they were so quiet I looked to see who they were, but

" Broken was the golden bowl,
The spirit flown forever."

CHAPTER XVIII.

"The eyes of women and lips of men
Welcome the soldiers of battles ten,
Coming back to their homes again
Sobered, but not dismayed."

AKERS.

IT was discovered early in the morning of the 19th of September that Lee's army had crossed the river into Virginia. I rode by request with Generals Franklin, Smith, and Brooks over the route of our charge to describe it to them. In a barn on the outskirts of Sharpsburg I found Corporal Johnson of Company G with his knee shattered. A stray surgeon came by, and calling him in to amputate the leg, I had my first experience in tying up arteries; but poor Johnson died on our hands.

Colonel Connor came up and joined us, nearly recovered from his severe illness. We were very glad to see him again, as well as some chickens he brought with him. I had fallen heir to Captain Morse's man, Bennett, who was the most perfect servant and the most expert forager I ever saw. Bennett soon had the chickens broiling, and our spirits rose from the depression caused by our losses as we indulged once more in a civilized meal.

In a few days Colonel Mason returned, and his first official act was to put me in arrest, nominally for not having kept him informed of the doings of the regiment, but I did n't know where he was and " had other fish to fry." He soon repented and released me. His real reason was that I had recommended to the governor a lot of sergeants for promotion. I also caused all the vacancies in non-commissioned officers to be filled, and had written on each warrant, " For especial gallantry at Antietam." This had a very happy effect. The success of a regiment depends more on good non-commissioned officers than anything else, and I think they are not always selected with sufficient care, or made enough of. My idea then was to make bravery the only test for promotion, and the colonel preferred to advance men of cleanliness and faultless equipment. If you stimulate the pride of a brave man by promotion, he is almost sure to do you credit unless he is a drunkard, and it is singular, too, that the clean and careful soldier is also pretty sure to make a good officer. So both the colonel and I may have been right.

On the 4th of October, to our great joy, we received orders for home, which the annexed letter to Governor Washburn will explain : —

HEADQUARTERS ARMY OF THE POTOMAC,
CAMP NEAR SHARPSBURG, MD., October 4, 1862.

To His Excellency the Governor of the State
of Maine:

SIR, — In view of the reduced and shattered condition of the Seventh Regiment of Maine Volunteers, the result of arduous service and exposure during the campaigns on the Peninsula and in Maryland, I made on the 2d inst. a special application to the War Department that the regiment should be sent to report to you in Maine, that it might be recruited and reorganized under your personal supervision. I yesterday received the necessary authority, as you will observe by the copy of the Special Order No. 271 from these headquarters, inclosed herein. I send the regiment to you for the purpose indicated. I beg that when this purpose shall have been accomplished, that the regiment may be ordered to report to me with all practical dispatch.

In returning this gallant remnant of a noble body of men, whose bravery has been exhibited on every field almost in the campaigns cited, to the State whose pride it is to have sent them forth, I feel happy that it has been in my power to signify, even in this insufficient manner, my appreciation of their services and of their value to this army, and I will venture on the latter

GENERAL GEORGE B. MC CLELLAN

account to ask your Excellency's best endeavors to fill at once their diminished ranks, that I may again see their standard in the Army of the Potomac. I am, with much respect,

Your obedient servant,

(Signed) GEO. B. McCLELLAN,

Major-General, U. S. A.

A leave of absence for the winter! Visions of home, of sleigh rides, skating parties, and the prettiest girls in America, in our opinion, rose before us.

Our ranks had been filled by the return of the convalescents, so, as we filed out of camp to take the cars at Hagerstown, we were nearly as strong as when we charged Lee's army.

Two pictures of the homeward journey only remain,— our march, the whole length of Broadway through cheering crowds and the booming of saluting cannon, and the hearty entertainment given us by the city of Boston. George S. Hillard made the speech of welcome, and the Board of Aldermen dined the officers at Parker's, and our men at the Hancock House. A paper of that date says of Captain Channing, "He relates many touching and heroic incidents." Some of us happened to overhear him telling a lot of people on the steps of the Parker House that " we had fifty men so badly wounded at Antietam we had to kill them," and he was chaffed so, he took a quick leave of absence to his home at Kendall's Mills.

But our great reception was to come when we reached Portland. I quote from the " Portland Press ": " Before the soldiers left the cars, ladies were passing at the side, distributing beautiful bouquets among them. As they emerged from the station, shouts of welcome rent the air. The cheering was most vociferous, and salutes were fired from field-pieces near by. The officers and soldiers looked worn-out with hardships and privations they had suffered."

We were escorted to the City Hall by the 17th regulars, the 23d, 25th, and 27th Maine regiments under the command of General Francis Fessenden, and by all the civic bodies. When we came upon the platform, I saw the tall form of Speaker Reed, on leave from the Navy, leading the cheers. Governor Washburn received us, and every word of his speech went to our hearts, especially the following, for soldiers are as susceptible to flattery as other people : " It was in a struggle for human rights on that dreadful day at Antietam that your little but devoted band, by its gallantry, courage, and consecration, made for itself a name that shall live so long as the memory of this war remains, and won from its division commander the exalted praise that it had performed the 'most gallant feat of arms he had ever seen or heard of or read in history.' "

And then we were surfeited with banquets and kind welcomings, the recollection of which is not dimmed by years. In the festivities of that happy winter we missed the great battle of Fredericksburg on the Rappahannock, where Burnside's lack of ability caused the Army of the Potomac a useless repulse and the loss of twelve thousand men. Our division did not happen to be much engaged, so they did not lose much, but it seemed to us as if we should have been there ; and when the order came for five full companies, and the lieutenant-colonel and major to take the field, we were ready and anxious to go.

We really wanted to go back, and why men should want to seek out hardship and danger, I cannot explain, but it must have been because we had not yet had enough of it. We would have hardly felt the same in the gloomy days of Cold Harbor yet to come. I had told Governor Washburn how Sergeant Henry F. Hill had got me out of the orchard at Antietam, and asked for his promotion. To my joy, the warm-hearted little governor made him captain, and no better captain was in our army till he met his death at Spottsylvania. Colonel Mason had drilled and disciplined his men in fine shape that winter, so when our battalion started for the front, we were very proud of our appearance, though the parting with sweethearts, and wives, and mothers had grieved us sore.

I had found a good deal of secession feeling in my native town, which I never have been able to understand. They were all kind to me personally, but why any Northern man or woman should sympathize with the South was then, and is now, a riddle impossible of solution. We knew little of politics in the army, and men of all shades of opinion were united with the single thought of putting down the rebellion, and among the rank and file there was never to my knowledge any doubt that they would accomplish it.

CHAPTER XIX.

"Nothing can cover his high fame but heaven:
　　No pyramids set off his memories,
But the eternal substance of his greatness:
　　To which I leave him."

BEAUMONT AND FLETCHER.

AGAIN in the comfortless and slow-moving trains we are off to Washington; again the sweet and quaint Quaker hospitality of Philadelphia moves our hearts; and again we disembark at the old station at the Capital. The doors of our favorite Metropolitan Hotel are open wide, and, among the throngs of people in blue, we find friend after friend. Then came the damp and snowy trip to Aquia Creek, and a long march in the mud to get to the old brigade. There we found a right royal welcome.

The weather and the roads forbade any early opening of the campaign. It was now February, and at least three months must elapse before there was any pressing need of our services. As I realized this, and discovered I had been sent to the field by the colonel's own sweet will, and as five companies did not need two field officers, I began not to like it much. I was probably a little spoiled by commanding the regiment so long, and, as I was an entirely unnecessary functionary where I was, I concluded to take no chances of serving under Colonel M. again. I could get along with every one else, but not with him. I will not detail the reasons. He had many fine qualities, and now holds high rank in the regular army, but an irrepressible conflict had broken out between us.

General William B. Franklin had been relieved from the command of the left grand division, and General William F. Smith reigned in his stead. General Franklin had fallen under the displeasure of the authorities in Washington as a friend of McClellan. As a commander of troops he proved himself cool and brave, and of great ability. No one then serving in the army could have commanded it better. Could McClellan's mantle have fallen upon him instead of upon Burnside, there would have been a different "making of splendid names," but he was loyal to his friend, as well as his country, and fate, in irony, suffered him, like Sedgwick, to appear before the country as a scapegoat for an incompetent commanding general. It was but for a moment, however; like Sedgwick, he was soon acquitted by public opinion. Time has spared him to be one of the most notable living figures of the war, and it is the prayer of the

GENERAL W. B. FRANKLIN

survivors of the 6th corps that he may live for many years their most distinguished comrade, their honored and trusted leader.

I went to headquarters, saw General " Baldy " Smith, and told him of my woes. He said, "I am disappointed that you did not come back in command of a Maine regiment. I will detail you as acting inspector-general on my staff." To this were added the little courtesies that so please an inferior when coming from one exalted in rank. " Baldy " Smith was a kind man to his subordinates, and had the soul of a great soldier in him. He was, at times, a perfect Ishmaelite to his superior officers, as they found out to their cost. I have seen him handle his division in a way that Napoleon would have loved, and yet sometimes, when the pall of superior authority fell over him, he was a dreadful kicker. He wrecked the chance of a greater name in these ways. Still, he was so kind to me when he commanded forty thousand men — to me, still a boy with all a boy's freshness and belief in everybody — that he ranks yet in my mind among the greatest commanders of the war.

With great delight, I assumed, to me, the proud position of Inspector-General Left Grand Division, vice Colonel O. E. Babcock absent on leave (afterward of Grant's staff).

I first went into a little mess presided over

by one Trundy, excelling in soups and the broiled birds of the country. Colonel McMahon, adjutant-general; Colonel Tolles, chief quartermaster; Colonel Platt, and Captain Platt his brother, were my chums. Poor Tolles! killed after he had surrendered, by Mosby's men in the later days, — so sweet-natured and so able! McMahon soon became my idol. Born of Irish ancestry, and wonderfully educated by the Jesuits, of high and chivalrous aims, he was the Chevalier Bayard of the corps, and wherever one of the 6th corps now dwells, does he not remember and love McMahon? Colonel Platt was an old regular, and I don't remember what unkind fate prevented his being a major-general, but he was not, and he has gone where it is said faithful and modest service is recorded. Captain Platt had the forceful ability which should have commanded a higher rank, and he has since made his mark as a member of Congress from Virginia, and as a great industrial pioneer in the far West. All these gentlemen were very kind to the newcomer, and happiness came to dwell within my tent. Soon an order came abolishing the left grand division, and ordering General John Sedgwick to command the 6th corps. I began to tremble for fear I would be ordered back to my regiment: it was not because I loved the regiment less, however. One day a grizzled, bluff major-general rode up to our quarters with an aide-de-camp as handsome as Romeo, and General S. dismounted and disappeared in General Smith's tent. I took the bull by the horns immediately and told Captain W. my tale, and was detailed the next day as provost marshal general of the corps. This office I found on inquiry was a very important one. I had charge of the police and discipline of twenty thousand men, and of all matters of trade, secret intelligence, home communication, and also of civil relations with people within our lines.

CHAPTER XX.

"Seeking the bubble reputation
Even in the cannon's mouth."

SHAKESPEARE.

THE winter of '62 and '63 was marked by the hard work of organizing and improving the army. Constant drills, reviews, and inspections followed each other. Our camp was at White Oak Church, on the high grounds overlooking the Rappahannock and the distant spires of Fredericksburg. This little church was a small, plain, unpainted structure, devoid of steeple or belfry, such an edifice as that in which "the blind preacher" officiated, but it gave its name to an important post office that winter. The coming of the mail was the most notable event in camp life, and we considered Jimmy Williams, the mail carrier, about the best-looking man in those parts; he was even better looking than the paymaster. Ex-Governor Robie was our paymaster all through the war, and when he came to camp the fatted calf of our simple hospitality was killed, fresh pine boughs were strewn for his repose, and we received the welcome greenbacks at his hands, thinking little about their market value so long as they defrayed mess or sutler's bills.

But the time was drawing near for action; the red muddy roads were drying up, the discipline and morale of the army were about perfect, confidence in Hooker was unbounded, and when we moved out of our dismantled winter homes we felt that the war was going to be ended this time.

And what an interesting drama war seemed to me as my vision of it unfolded from the staff-officer's standpoint. No more confinement to the dusty column, no more ignorance of what is going on, but all the business possessed of interest or pageantry was mine; and it had its drawbacks too, for while the 7th Maine were in quiet bivouac, we were riding back and forth all night carrying messages to old General Benham of the engineers who was laying the pontoon bridges over the river in darkness, fog, and musketry fire. In the morning our corps and the 1st crossed with just enough opposition to make some excitement, and when the sun cleared away the fog, the view of some fifty thousand men, the distant skirmishers in touch with the enemy, our magnificent batteries going into position as if by clockwork, and all the banners of the Greek Cross flaunting in the breeze, made a picture that has survived many

years. We know now that Jackson begged to
be allowed to attack us, and promised Lee to
drive us into the river, but he rode along his
lines, got a good look, changed his mind, and
went gunning for the 11th corps.

The 1st corps now left to join Hooker's
main army at Chancellorsville, and all that day
we waited expecting an attack, but none came.
Some of us turned in at dark in a ruined house
by the river, and were waked up near midnight
to find our orders had come.   General Sedgwick
was directed to move up the river to Fredericksburg, take the Heights, and to move out some
fifteen miles from Fredericksburg to attack Lee's
rear by daylight.   We were about four miles
from Fredericksburg, the corps was in line of
battle facing the enemy, and it was pitch-dark.
However, as soon as the orders could be distributed to the divisions, we got under way and
moved up the river road, with occasional halts
for the troops to catch up, and other halts to attack and drive away the felt but unseen enemy,
and I remember how queer the skirmish fire
looked in the mist and darkness. I had ar-
ranged my business of provost marshal so my
presence in the rear was not needed, and had
asked General Sedgwick for permission to serve
as one of his aides-de-camp. This he granted
with a pleased twinkle in his eye, and I look on

it now as my proudest distinction that I was enabled to so serve with him while he lived. Toward daylight, just as the mists were beginning to look ghastly in the coming light, the head of our column reached Fredericksburg, and pushed through the edge of the town toward the Heights. We were expected to have taken them, and to have been some fifteen miles farther on at this time by army headquarters, but they were expecting more than could be done, had General Early been elsewhere.

He was not only there, but extremely obstinate about getting away from there, as we found to our cost. It was impossible to tell whether the Heights were occupied by the enemy or not, on account of the fog through which, once in a while, the sounds were ominous. Two regiments moved off toward the hill in line, and they were soon swallowed up in the mist into which the general and all of us were eagerly peering.

Then came the familiar whistling of bullets about us and a crackling fire in the unknown beyond, and then the sudden lifting of the watery curtain for an instant revealed to us the intrenched lines full of men, and our two regiments giving back with heavy loss.

"For God's sake, rally those men," broke from the general's lips as he pulled his slouch hat lower over his eyes. With the best speed of good horses, riding up the hill where Burnside's thousands fell, some of us were with our breaking line in less time than it takes to tell it, and soon had them re-formed behind a favorable piece of ground. The experience was not pleasant, however, of being fired at personally by as many Southern marksmen as took a notion. I can see Kent now, his whiskers streaming, his blue overcoat up round his ears, and his revolver brandished in the air. He was wounded soon after in not half so hard a place as this.

The mist fell again, and it was quite friendly to us this time, for we withdrew the line, and then every effort was made to get the corps up in position for an assault, which was the only thing left to do.

It was not a cheering prospect, for the works before us were the same Burnside had failed to take with three corps. They were full of men now, and there were no more behind them then. Till nearly ten o'clock we rode back and forth with orders; then every one seemed to be in place and have his instructions. We had our headquarters in a yard on one of the streets in town looking up toward the Heights. The several commanders had received their orders from General Sedgwick in person, and had started to join their commands, when the first shot from Marye's Hill was fired. Afterward I asked the captain of the New Orleans Washington artillery who fired it, and he said, "Corporal ——, the best shot in the Southern army, sir."

There was a Napoleon gun in the street: this it stripped of cannoneers; then it killed a major of artillery near by; killed McMahon's horse as he was mounting; passed me by; put two holes through Kent's arm and eleven through his overcoat as he lay asleep in the yard, and wounded several men and horses in our cavalry escort behind. So much damage could a well-directed spherical case inflict. Henry Farrar of Bangor had just joined our staff as a volunteer aide, and as soon as we were all mounted, which the spherical case had somewhat hastened, General Sedgwick said, "Now, young gentlemen, here is a chance for you to distinguish yourselves by leading the storming columns." Farrar started at once, new horse, uniform, and all, but I pursued him and told him the general was joking, and he ever after gave me the credit of saving his life. It is said of old Colonel Burnham of the 6th Maine, who commanded the light division, to whom was given the post of honor in the assault, that when he left General Sedgwick and rode down to his command, who were lying in ditches and other cover outside the town, he said, " Boys, I have got a government contract." " What is it, Colonel ? " came from all along his line. " One thousand rebels, potted and salted, and got to have 'em in less than five minutes. Forward! guide centre! " He got them.

CHAPTER XXI.

"Lo! the Ammonites thicken and onward they come."

MOTHERWELL.

"A bed nor comfortless, nor new
To him who took his rest whene'er
The hour arrived, no matter where."

BYRON.

WHEN the two assaulting columns and the line of battle moved upon Marye's Heights, I started to go up with the right attack, which was on the county road, and was composed of four regiments in column of fours. Colonel Spear and the 61st Pennsylvania were in the lead and received nearly the whole fire from the enemy's intrenchments and batteries. Colonel Spear was killed, and the loss was so heavy and sudden that the column was checked and thrown into confusion in the narrow road, down which grape-shot seemed to be searching for everybody. We all worked hard to get into shape again, and went forward, when, to my joy, I saw that the stars and stripes were planted on the enemy's works, and beyond them could see butts of muskets whirling in the air where the 6th Maine and 5th Wisconsin were engaged in a brief hand to hand fight. The green slope was dotted all over with still forms in blue, and the prisoners were streaming down the hill in hundreds. Remembering it was my duty as provost marshal to take care of the prisoners, I soon had some fifteen hundred collected in town. Among them were the officers of the Washington artillery, who had very fine horses that they particularly commended to my care. I thought I took pains to take care of them, as I left them in good hands in the town, but they were recaptured the next day. It was in a high state of exhilaration that we started forward, for with about six thousand men we had taken the place Burnside had hurled so many divisions against, in vain, the preceding December. Its defenders were about the same in number too, for the earthworks were full on both occasions. We moved on southwest toward Chancellorsville several miles, meeting opposition occasionally, and listening anxiously for the sound of firing from the main army. None was heard, however, and near Salem Church the Confederates were found in force. We attacked with varying success, but finally were repulsed by constantly increasing numbers, and darkness fell before our attack could be renewed. An ominous rumbling of wheels was the only sound that broke the stillness. This

showed that the enemy were diligently reinforcing from Lee's army, which was between us and
Hooker, and the entire absence of all sounds of
battle or any communication from Chancellorsville was most strange and ill boding. General
Sedgwick sat all night by the roadside just behind Williston's battery, and the corps was faced
in three directions, forward, to our left, and back
toward Fredericksburg, as the enemy had moved
in behind us and reoccupied the Heights. Oh
for the sound of one gun off toward the Wilderness, where three fourths of our army were! It
was so evident that we were being surrounded
by greatly superior forces. Morning broke gray
and pale. We could, perhaps, get communication with Hooker by Banks's Ford, off to our
right and rear where the engineers under General Benham were guarding the bridges they had
laid. Colonel Tompkins was sent there with a
message. He did not return. Captain Farrar
was sent. He came back to us some months
after by way of Richmond and exchange. Then
General Sedgwick in impatience sent me. I did
not take the road, but took a beeline across
country, most fortunately, for I was back in
an hour, having seen no wandering rebels.

In the forenoon Early attacked our second
(Howe's) division from the direction of Fredericksburg. The 7th Maine and 49th New York

were on the skirmish line and repulsed the attack, taking two hundred prisoners, and Corporal Boston of the 7th took the flag of the 58th Virginia. The day wore on slowly, and still no firing from Chancellorsville. Word came from Hooker " to look to the safety of the corps," that he " was too far off to direct." The enemy's forces were evidently still increasing and moving around us. We did not know then that General Lee in person was marshaling McLaw's, Early's, and Anderson's divisions, to make a crushing attack upon us from the side of Fredericksburg, but we knew an attack was coming soon from somewhere.

In the afternoon I went over to see the regiment, and found them in the first line of Howe's division. I was sitting on the ground with Colonel Connor and Channing, talking over the chances of the fight, for we were skirmishing in three directions, and, pulling out my watch, I said, " It is quarter of five ; if they are coming it will be before five o'clock," when the rebel yell broke from the woods far in front, and the whole hillside was alive with men. It was a gallant sight ! They came on in three lines, about 16,000 strong, and were so near that regimental, brigade, and division commanders with their staffs could be plainly seen. Our brigade was commanded then by General Neill, called " Beau Neill " in the old army. I saw him draw his little sword as de-

CAPTAIN H. W. FARRAR, A. D. C.

liberately and gracefully as if at West Point on parade, and then make the dreadful mistake of giving the order " Forward ! 3d brigade ! " We were in a beautiful position on the hillside, but down we charged into the ravines below that had already broken the formation of our numerous enemy. I took the right of the regiment, and it was soon cut in two, we going down one ravine and Colonel Connor down the other. General Neill and staff were all *hors de combat* and Colonel Connor wounded in less time than it takes to tell it, and the little brigade had smashed itself to pieces against ten times its numbers. Our batteries were firing over our heads, and the smoke obscured everything, but I saw the trend of the attack was toward our left and Banks's Ford.

As the smoke lifted, I saw rebels near me on both sides, and moved by a desire to avoid capture, and also to warn our batteries of their danger, I ran my horse to the rear, and was obliged to pass through Rigby's battery, where the smoke obscured everything so I could not tell if I were running into their fire or not. I remember this as a particularly unpleasant sensation, but fortunately for me I got between the guns unscathed in time for the battery to limber up and away, and to my joy I saw our second line, the Vermonters, were as firm as a rock, and that the attack was wearing itself out on them and on the 5th Wisconsin and other troops to their left just brought over by Colonel McMahon. As so many of the enemy seemed to be going toward Banks's Ford, our only line of retreat, I thought the general ought to know it, and went to him as fast as my horse could go, hatless and breathless. He and General Newton were standing in the road and moved toward me as I came in sight, and the general asked me at once, " What force is attacking us ? " " About as many as our corps showed on the last review," said I, and General Newton smiled an incredulous smile. General Sedgwick then directed me to General Wheaton's brigade and told me to conduct him to reinforce Howe. I did so, and we got there in time to fire a few shots, but the great attack had spent its force, was fairly repulsed, and we had a large number of prisoners. This attack had about as many men in it as Pickett's attack at Gettysburg, and was directed by General Lee in person. Why it did not succeed is hard to tell. It was certainly gallantly resisted and defeated by a third of its numbers. The ground over which it was directed was very much broken with ravines, and I think the different generals may have tried to reorganize their disjointed commands until it was too late to go on, on account of the darkness falling. It is amusing now to read the reports of the Confederate generals engaged, and see how unanimous they seem to have been in the idea that they then and there broke us and drove us over Banks's Ford, when the only broken troops on our side were Neill's brigade, smashed like a pitcher thrown against a rock, by charging nine rebel brigades, and when some hours later the corps marched leisurely to Banks's Ford in obedience to an order of General Hooker, and crossed there with all its property on wheels.

The nights about that time were all foggy and misty, and this was no exception. When we got down near the pontoon bridges, we found the enemy thought he had their range and was dropping shells toward them from several directions. The firing was like so many graceful curves of rockets, but not a bridge, animal, or man was hit. Captain Pierce, our signal officer, and I crossed the bridge together, and, absolutely weary, about two in the morning we found a place in the woods to hide for a nap. No sooner were we stowed away comfortably than the horrid screech of a shell would seem to be searching for us, and Pierce would get up on his elbow and say, " Tom, where did that strike ? " and then we would move. How many times we moved, I don't know, but we seemed to be still moving in our dreams when we awoke after daylight in a pouring rainstorm and found much of the corps had marched over us and taken all our little movables, as mementos, doubtless. Both we and our horses, wet, hungry, tired, and wretched, chanced on a Samaritan when we found Dr. Ash at his hospital.

The disastrous campaign of Chancellorsville was over, and we soon learned that Hooker was trying to make Sedgwick and the 6th corps his scapegoat, when we had lost nearly as many men, and taken more prisoners, colors, and guns than all the rest of the army together.

CHAPTER XXII.

"On his bold visage middle age
Had slightly pressed its signet sage."

SCOTT.

IT was with chagrin and disappointment that we tramped back in the mud to our old camps at White Oak Church, and proceeded to get them into living shape again. Tents were soon stretched over the stockades, fresh evergreens were cut, and we began to take stock of our blessings and misfortunes. Hope, never taking a long flight from youth, came again on the balmy air of the Southern spring. What if Hooker had lost his head? What if the 11th corps had failed to stand the attack of three times their numbers? What if Lee with half its force had compelled the Army of the Potomac to recross the river, — were not the shot-torn banners of the 6th corps waving as proudly as ever? Who now or hereafter, friend or foe, could criticise our fighting or our fame? The fortified works of the enemy had been stormed at the point of the bayonet; prisoners, guns, and colors had been taken, and an assault of half Lee's army, led by Lee in person, had been repelled by half our corps! This was glory enough for our young hearts, and we began to be eager for the time when we could meet the enemy again, could it only be under a general who equaled the ability on the other side.

I had guards at most of the houses down the Rappahannock for ten miles outside our lines, and it was delightful to visit them again after a keen morning's gallop, and to be courteously greeted sometimes by ladies of Virginia's first families who could appreciate our care of their property. This was a debatable ground, but the Southern soldiers knew our peaceful errands and never molested us. Sometimes, while riding on the river-bank, a tall, lank rebel dressed in "butternut" would step out from his picket post in the woods across the river and gravely present arms, while I scrupulously returned the salute. Sometimes another would "draw a bead" on me in joke, but a pleasant salutation always brought the gun down. At such times it was easy to realize that they were our fellow-countrymen, if misguided; but in the press of battle they were foemen, — nothing more.

At this camp we built of evergreen fence a riding course, and under the guidance of Captain Beaumont of our staff, afterwards instructor in horsemanship at West Point, and lately colonel of the 4th regular cavalry, some of

us passed hours daily shooting at a mark,
or cutting with the sabre at mimic heads,
when at full speed. With our horses on the
run we could pick up a handkerchief from the
ground, and we emulated all the tricks of the
frontiersman or the Mexican vaquero. This
practice stood us in good stead often in the
years of fighting that were to follow. General
Sedgwick, always kind and indulgent as a father
to the young men on his staff, sympathized in
all our sports, and his presence made the game
or the race, or even the cockfight, more interesting. This year, while the survivors of these
young men were, on Memorial Day, reverently
kneeling by his grave at Cornwall Hollow, I
read upon the tombstone, —

"JOHN SEDGWICK,
KILLED MAY 9, 1864,
AGED 51 YEARS."

— and I remember how we used to think of
him as "old Uncle John." Fifty-one years does
not seem old, does it, comrades?

The Southern army, reinforced and swelling
with honest pride, were even now stretching
out to their left toward the Blue Ridge, and
it was the inception of another invasion of the
North. We were ordered to lay the pontoon

bridges and cross the river again to see who was left over there. It was done, and for days we went through all the actual work of warfare with but little fighting. There was a good deal of lively cannonading, and I remember the rebels had a Whitworth gun that they fired from such a distance that neither its smoke nor explosion could be perceived, and its presence was only announced by the scream of the steel projectile as it went whistling by. Farrar said one day, "General, I would like to know if there is anything you are afraid of." The general replied, "I don't like these Whitworth bolts."

It was now demonstrated that A. P. Hill's corps were alone at Fredericksburg, that Jackson was in the Valley, and Longstreet following after, so then began another series of marches toward Washington and Maryland. Here I learned one of the pleasant little duties that sometimes fall to a staff officer's lot, after perhaps twelve hours in the saddle, when the route happens to be through a friendly country. The troops are going wearily into camp. "Major, we march to Frying Pan Shoals to-morrow, about twenty miles : this map is wretched. Go there, acquaint yourself with the road and the best places to halt for water, and be back here by daybreak." Then on another horse, through the dark woods, through the blinding rain, with a colored man for guide, nothing but blackness visible, which is well, for no guerrillas will be abroad, I press on all the lonely night and take my place in the marching column again at dawn, to traverse again the same road. Staff duty was no sine-cure, though no doubt it seemed so to our bre-thren of the line, as we dashed by on good horses, sometimes guilty of a " boiled shirt," and often attaining a square meal at a farmhouse distant from the column, while our orderlies kept watch and ward. But our duty was never finished. When the regimental officers were lying down by the fire and smoking a last pipe before turning in, we were on our way to some other corps or to army headquarters to get or give information, or we were making ready in various ways for the march and fight to-morrow. With all this, I look back on it as a charming experience. Its sorry features are dimmed by distance, and of all my earlier years it is difficult to imagine any more enjoyable than these spent on the staff of the 6th army corps.

We skirted Washington on our march north-ward, and the adventures of those who skipped off and went there were celebrated in song and story. I visited at Fairfax the camps of some new Maine regiments, and received a most cor-dial greeting from Colonels Francis Fessenden and T. H. Hubbard.

We crossed into Maryland at Edward's Ferry. About this time the command of the army had been offered to General Sedgwick, but he declined it, advising the choice of either Meade or Reynolds. When the news came that Meade was selected, I remember the general struck his spurs into his gigantic and phlegmatic steed and led us at quite a pace for some time. Whatever emotion he may have felt on the subject was vented in this way. His only regret, however, was on our account, for we were all ambitious to be on the staff of the army. I was sent to Frederick City with dispatches, and arrived just in time to see General Hooker turn over the command to General Meade. Hooker never appeared better than on this occasion. He admirably became the high position he was laying down on account of a vagary of the military crank who happened to command the armies of the United States. Halleck had refused him the garrison of Harper's Ferry, then utterly useless for anything else. After Meade took command, it was given him without question. Meade in his well-worn uniform, splashed with mud, with his glasses, and his nervous and earnest air, looked more like a learned pundit than a soldier, but he at once informed himself of the position of the army and took the reins in that business-like fashion he so well maintained till the end.

CHAPTER XXIII.

" And his low headcrest, just one sharp ear bent back
For my voice, and the other pricked out on his track;
And one eye's black intelligence, — ever that glance
O'er its white edge at me, his own master, askance;
And the thick heavy spume flakes, which aye and anon
His fierce lips shook upward in galloping on."

ROBERT BROWNING.

ON the 30th of June, 1863, the 6th army corps reached the pretty little town of Manchester, Md., distant about twenty miles from the headquarters of the army, then at Taneytown, and thirty-six miles from Gettysburg, towards which columns of both armies were directed, themselves ignorant of each other's vicinage. It was fine summer weather, and the young gentlemen of the staff improved the next day by making the acquaintance of the fair Union ladies of the place.

At five in the afternoon, the general wanted to send an officer to General Meade's headquarters for orders and information, and, as I happened to be about, I was chosen. With an orderly I rode twenty miles to Taneytown through a beautiful country, the air filled with the scent of flowers and new-mown hay.

Near Taneytown I came upon General Hancock riding to headquarters from the field, and he told me of the gallant fight of the 1st corps that day, how they had been defeated by greater numbers at last, how General Reynolds had been killed, and of the new line formed in the Cemetery of Gettysburg. Soon we saw the headquarters tents glimmering in the darkness, and I reported to General Seth Williams, adjutant-general of the army, who gave me some refreshments, and told me there was a council of war going on in General Meade's large hospital tent next to his. After waiting awhile, he took me in, and I saw General Meade in the centre standing by a table covered with maps, and several corps commanders grouped around. There was Howard, with his empty sleeve, commanding the 11th corps; Sickles, commanding the 3d corps; Slocum, commanding the 12th corps; and Sykes, commanding the 5th corps, besides Hancock. General Meade, after finishing a remark he was making in a low voice when I entered, said, "To-morrow, gentlemen, we fight the decisive battle of the war. Where is the officer from the 6th corps?" As I stepped forward, he handed me, written on yellow tissue paper, the orders for the corps, and another for General Newton to take command of the 1st corps. He told me to commit them to memory

GENERAL GEORGE G. MEADE

and destroy them in case of need, as the enemy's cavalry were reported scouting about. He then asked me if I had a cavalry escort; when I told him I had not, he offered me one. I told him I would get through quicker alone. He then said, "Tell General Sedgwick that I expect to put him in on the right, and hope he will be up in time to decide the victory for us."

General Meade's solemn bearing impressed me very much, and I felt some awe at the circumstances in which I was placed, being little more than a boy in age. Near midnight I started on my return, feeling as if I had something to do with the fate of the nation. After a long gallop, I came upon farmers driving off their horses, who told me that Stuart's cavalry was just behind them, and I kept a bright lookout, several times hiding in the woods and waiting till mounted men got by, whose hoof-beats were plainly audible in the still night. I don't think I passed any rebels, though, for their cavalry was, unfortunately for Lee, cut off from our rear. However, I did not know that, and, as I was hiding again about three in the morning and holding my horse's nose, instead of some of Mosby's gentry I saw General Sedgwick's straw hat appear through the trees at the head of the corps. General Newton was riding with him, and I delivered the orders. Now General

Sedgwick, hearing of the battle, had started the corps for Taneytown, and the orders were to take the Baltimore Pike for Gettysburg, thirty-six miles away.

If anything had happened to me that night, he would have gone on to Taneytown, taking two sides of the triangle instead of one. We should have made something like fifty miles instead of thirty-six. We then could not have arrived on the second day, which might have changed the fate of the battle, for eighteen thousand troops not coming up would probably have made a difference in the memorable council of war held on the night of the second day, and the question, " Shall the Army of the Potomac fight here ? " have been answered differently. We all like to think ourselves of some use, and such were my youthful speculations.   General Sedgwick, though unusually stern and quiet, gave me a kind word, and we turned the head of the column to make a cross-cut of a few miles to the Baltimore Pike.   Then began one of the hardest marches we ever knew — thirty-six miles in dust and unusual heat ; but the men pressed on with vigor and courage through it all, feeling themselves on Northern soil again and feeling that we were expected to decide the victory. My continuous ride was over seventy miles when we stopped behind the circle of hills over which the cannon smoke was rising and where many a little white cloud, almost resting in the air, showed each where a rebel shell had burst.

While we had been toiling along the Baltimore Pike so many weary miles, many men with feet bleeding and scarcely a man falling out, we had heard no news. We were aware that our people were engaged only by the booming of the artillery which sounded strangely muffled coming from behind the horseshoe of hills that made the Union position.

CHAPTER XXIV.

"Through the long tormented air
  Heaven flashed a sudden jubilant ray,
  And down we swept and charged and overthrew."
  TENNYSON.

THE beautiful dawn of the second day of the
battle looked upon the bulk of both great armies
in readiness for action : the Confederates about
seventy thousand strong, the Union army about
eighty thousand, marshaled against each other
in grim array. Our people had a circular position with the bow toward the enemy. The
rugged sides of Culp's Hill formed the right,
the gentle slopes and plateau of the cemetery
the centre, and behind our left which was, later
in the day, pushed out to the Emmetsburg Pike
by General Sickles, frowned Great and Little
Round Top. The Confederate line enveloped
ours, and that became one of their chief disad-
vantages in the fight, as the distances were
greater going around their half-circle with orders
or reinforcements, — very much greater than ours
were to take a radius, or an arc, of our circle.
The unconnected nature of many of their
attacks may thus be accounted for. Both sides

spent much of the forenoon manœuvring for position. But Lee organized two forward movements, one on our right at Culp's Hill and the cemetery by Ewell ; and the other by Longstreet with Hood's Texas division and McLaw's, intended to outflank our left. Both were expected to have been delivered earlier in the day, and much recrimination has been indulged in by the Southern generals since on this subject. The attack upon Culp's Hill, which formed the right of our line, was furious in the extreme, but after some hours of fight, when darkness fell, the only advantage gained by the Confederates was the possession of a part of the line of the 12th corps, they being unaware that they had almost reached the Baltimore Pike, where were our trains, hospitals, and ammunition wagons.

Longstreet's attack, if delayed, was magnificent, even as his attack at Chickamauga was magnificent. There was an angle in our line on Sickles's front. Longstreet put his whole force at this angle, near which was the celebrated Peach Orchard, and doubled Sickles back on the 2d corps in one direction and toward Devil's Den and Little Round Top in the other. During this part of the action and the fighting which followed, the 3d, 4th, 17th, 19th, and the 20th Maine regiments did great honor to the Pine Tree State.

Little Round Top, the possession of which meant victory to the Confederates, was only occupied by a signal officer at the time, who kept waving his flag at Hood's Texans struggling through Devil's Den and its rocky approaches to gain the coveted hill. Fortunately for our cause, General Warren, engineer in chief of the army, happened to ride up, and, seeing the gravity of the situation, got hold of Vincent's brigade of the 5th corps and Hazlitt's battery, and gained the summit, dragging the guns up by hand, and were just in time to hurl the Texans back in a bloody hand to hand struggle. In the mean time, Hill had become engaged on the Confederate side, and part of the 2d corps and all of the 5th corps on ours. General Sedgwick and his chief of staff, Colonel McMahon, had gone to Meade's headquarters for orders. Two of us had purchased some cherry-pies of a very freckled-faced girl at a neighboring farmhouse, and had just joined the rest of the staff, who were in the shadiest place they could find upon the banks of Rock Creek, and we were all listening with suppressed excitement to a tremendous outburst of cannon and musketry over the hills to the left, when McMahon came riding down the hill, swinging his hat and shouting, "The general directs the corps toward the heavy firing." In an instant

every man was on his feet. The fences were
broken down and the heads of the brigades
broke off into the fields and began ascending
the long slopes toward the Round Tops, nearly
a mile away. Captain Farrar and I were with
the first brigade to arrive (Colonel Nevins's), and
we all helped to swing it into line, as it moved
gallantly over the crest. General Sedgwick
sent us in with it, and as we went over the crest
the round shot whistled very close, and we
passed over what seemed to be fragments of the
5th corps, passed General Sykes commanding it,
and on into the smoke beyond at the double-
quick down to a stone wall at the right and foot
of Little Round Top, and opened a rousing fire.
The attack of the enemy in front reminded me
then of the last wave on the beach, stopping and
being pushed up a little more and a little more
from behind. I was on the right of the brigade,
and rode across behind it, where I saw the
boulders piled on the top of Little Round Top,
and started to ride up there to see what I could.
I had to go fast across the front of the Pennsylvania Reserves, who were making a charge that
looked like a picture of a battle, and it looked
as if it were on me.

Then my active little horse, forgetting his seventy or eighty mile ride, took me up the steep
northwest side of Little Round Top, to where

Hazlitt's guns were still firing, though their commander was dead and the rocks seemed to be covered with corpses in light blue Zouave uniform. I afterwards learned that they were the 140th New York. On looking back I could see no enemy firing except by Devil's Den and in the valley, and I was told by an officer ensconced behind a boulder that I had better get out of that if I did not want to be picked off, as the bullets were flattening themselves against the rocks all about. So quickly over the hill I went; and found what was left of the regular brigade under Colonel Greene, and they looked like a small regiment. Speaking to one or two friends I rode back to General Sedgwick and was glad to rest, for the fighting was over on the left for that day. Our several brigades had been sent as reinforcements to different points, so our command was small. Gloomy reports kept coming in, and near dark Major Whittier, the general's confidential aide, told me we were going to march back twenty miles that night, and that the general was going to the headquarters to a council of war. Later, we gladly learned we were to stay where we were. With a blanket and something to eat, and after a soothing pipe, with our saddles for pillows and overcoats for bed and blankets, we were soon sleeping the dreamless sleep of youth and fatigue.

CHAPTER XXV.

"And louder than the bolts of heaven
Far flashed the red artillery."

CAMPBELL.

AT daybreak of the third day, General Slocum attacked those of Ewell's corps who had ob-
tained a lodgment in his lines, and with the assistance of two brigades, Neill's and Shaler's of the
6th corps, succeeded in driving them out and rec-
tifying his line. After breakfast I went over to
the right, passing through the cemetery, and
came to Power's Hills where General Slocum had
his headquarters. He asked me to stay with him
a while as he was short of staff officers, and soon
told me to take Neill's brigade, in which was
my regiment, the 7th Maine, over to a hill to
the right of our whole line. After a short march
we came to the hill, got into line, and advanced
toward its wooded summit, but when halfway
up were received with a severe fire. The men,
however, took the double-quick and soon drove
the enemy from the top. Our opponents proved
to be the advance of Johnson's division, who
were working their way round our right and

soon would have been on the Baltimore Pike,
which would have been in the highest degree
disastrous to us.   I then rode back to General
Slocum to report, and then to General Sedgwick, near Little Round Top.

It was becoming exceedingly hot, and it was
very uncertain what was to be done.   As it is one
of the first duties of a staff officer to get information, I went over to Little Round Top, finding
I could get to it from one side not exposed to
sharpshooters.   Near the summit I discovered a
little rocky crest where I could see out all over
that part of the field.   It was still occupied as a
signal station, and my old friend Ned Pierce was
signal officer.   As the firing began to grow
over beyond Devil's Den, I soon saw blue-coated
troopers through intervals in the trees, and they
were attacking the infantry of the Confederate
right.   They seemed, from sight and sound, to
have penetrated quite a distance into the enemy's
lines, but as the ground became opener it was
cruel to see them charging over fences and up to
the woods only to be destroyed by the deliberate
fire of the Southern rifle.   This was Farns-
worth's celebrated charge in which he fell with
glory.   Looking off farther to the right, there
seemed to have been a change in the appearance
of the enemy's lines since the day before, and,
borrowing a glass from the signal officer, I was

able to distinguish much moving about of troops and artillery, as well as to count over a hundred guns ranged in a semicircle and seemingly directed toward the centre of our line. Many of them were Napoleon guns of polished brass and were glistening in the sun. I could not see ours from where I was, and did not know that Hunt had concentrated McGilvery and Hazard and the artillery reserve in nearly as formidable an array to reply. About this time, Generals Meade and Warren came up on the rocks to take a look, and I dodged back to tell the general that it looked like a cannonade pretty soon. We were all sitting down somewhere at noontime, with our horses close by, and enjoying a simple lunch of hard-tack and coffee, when two guns were fired from the enemy's lines.

I remember we were in a field which had many boulders and some small trees in it. I concluded I did not want any more lunch, and got behind a boulder large enough to cover me and my horse, and in a little while it began. Such a cannonade was never heard on the continent of America, one hundred and thirty guns on the Confederate side and eighty on ours. The rebels seemed to be mostly firing by battery, and ours one at a time. The open ground behind our line was being torn up in every direction by the shells. Occasionally a caisson exploded, riderless horses were dashing about, and a throng of wounded were streaming to the rear. When the cannonade was at its height and every one of judgment was utilizing what cover he could find, I saw coming over the plain behind us, which was being beaten into dust in every direction by the enemy's shells, a man with a long beard and spectacles, wearing a brown linen duster. When he got a little nearer, I saw that he was our sutler's clerk and that he staggered in his gait. As he got pretty near me, a shell shrieked between us with more than usually fiendish noise, and he looked down at me, putting his hand up to his ear, and said, " Listen to the mocking bird." With the providential good fortune of drunken men, he had crossed for some distance in safety over ground upon which it seemed impossible for any living thing to remain a minute.

This cannonade lasted about an hour, and we all knew that it was intended as the prelude to an infantry attack, but where the attack would be was in doubt, as their fire did not seem to be concentrated on any particular part of our line. That is where they were in error, as the whole of their fire directed on the 2d corps would have given their attack a much better chance. We did not feel very anxious, however, as our men were hugging the ground and gripping their muskets in front; and were they not the

tried and true that stormed St. Marye's Heights
not long ago, and had never lost a color or a gun
to the enemy since they had first marched out
from their far Northern homes? Now the fire on
our side stopped, but for fifteen minutes yet the
one hundred and thirty Confederate guns belch
out flame. Hunt, chief of artillery, had ordered
our fire to cease, that the guns might cool to be
ready for the coming assault. The enemy
thought that they had silenced our fire, only to
be bitterly disappointed a little later. Then
suddenly all the firing ceased, and there was a
lull. The smoke clouds were rising on the opposite crest, the sunlight again glinting on the
long line of brass guns; but what was that gray
mass that seemed to be moving scarce distin-
guishable from the smoke wreaths about it? In
a moment there was little doubt what it was, for
on comes the wonderful Virginia infantry of
Pickett, and beyond the North Carolinians of
Pender and Pettigrew, and this side the large
brigade of Cadmus Wilcox. It was a thrilling
sight, and I thought of the great charges of the
French infantry at Wagram and Austerlitz that
I loved to read of in childhood. On they came:
it looked to me like three lines about a mile long
each, in perfect order. They crossed the Emmetsburg Pike, and our guns, eighty in all,
cool and in good shape, open first with shot and

then with shell.   Great gaps are made every second in their ranks, but the gray soldiers close up to the centre and the color-bearers jump to the front, shaking and waving the " Stars and Bars." And so they pass out of my sight for a few minutes, as Zeigler's Grove in front of our line shuts them off.   But a tremendous roar of musketry crashes out, and I know the big guns are firing grape and canister now.   And soon they appear again, and this time the colors are together like a little forest, but the men are dropping like leaves in autumn.   They pass our line, thousands of men in gray left yet, and I believe our centre is pierced: I could not see that they threw down their arms.   So, fast as I could ride, I went down there for information, as I knew the general would want to attack at once with all the 6th corps he could lay hands on.   But I soon saw to my great joy that we were victors still, and that the flower of the South had dashed themselves to pieces against the sturdy 2d corps alone.   I saw General Armistead, the Confederate leader, dying, and near him Cushing of the regular artillery, who had fired his last gun with one hand, though partly cut in two, holding his body together with the other.   Then I tried to ride over the field, but could not, for the dead and wounded lay too thick to guide a horse through them.   Then it occurred to me that our corps must have orders by this time to make a counter-attack, as the thing to do under the circumstances, so I got back again as fast as possible, but was soon sent with a message to General Slocum on the right. While there I heard firing to the north of Gettysburg and rode out beyond our lines to see what it was, and from a hill was fortunate enough to see the defeat of Stuart's cavalry by Gregg. All it looked like was a dust cloud with flakes of light in it as the sun shone upon the swinging sabres. Lee had ordered his cavalry to attack on our right about the same time as Pickett, and they would have done us vast mischief had they succeeded in beating our cavalry, while if Pickett's charge had succeeded, they would have been in position to have done us similar damage to the work of the Prussian cavalry at Waterloo.

Thus ended the battle of Gettysburg. Lee retreated the next day, and, though he fought with skill and determination for two years more, there was little doubt of the end when the last of his dauntless columns filed through Monterey Gap on their way to cross the Potomac.

CHAPTER XXVI.

"Friendly traitress, loving foe."
CHARLES LAMB.

MORNING arose, dreary and pale, upon the battle-field of Gettysburg. It would soon resemble a vast charnel-house, but the work of covering up the mangled, blackened clay, and caring for poor maimed humanity was busily going on. The depression following great excitement was upon us, and it seemed as if our army was about to do its usual waiting after a victory. Whether wise or not, we did wait all day, and the rain fell in torrents. This was one of the days we needed Sheridan. Not until the next afternoon did orders come for the 6th corps to lead in the pursuit. General Sedgwick sent Lieutenant Andrews and me to visit the rebel hospitals and estimate the number of their wounded. In this painful duty the time wore away, occasionally enlivened by the meeting of my companion and some fellow West Pointer of the Confederate army, and their struggles at first to be very angry with each other were amusing to me.

At nightfall we managed to lose our way,

though we had started out all right toward the noise of a distant cannonade where our corps were trying to force a mountain pass. We rode on until midnight utterly lost, and at length seeing many lights on a hill beyond, for a time we thought we were up with the enemy. Carefully reconnoitring, however, we got to a large house where some thirty of the country people were holding a jubilee over our victory. They had as yet seen no one from the Union army, and the most unbounded hospitality was pressed upon us. We soon tore ourselves away from this Capua, and, getting the right direction at last, caught up with our headquarters by daybreak. Things had been going wrong. The general was walking up and down in the middle of the road, full of unusual wrath. We reported, and were put to work at once in as hard riding as we could do for the rest of that dismal day. Toward night we came to a mountain afterward known in our annals as "Mount Misery." The road lay directly over its summit, rocky and narrow. By midnight the head of our column reached the cloudy top in profound darkness and storm. The troops filled the steep highway which was fast becoming a torrent, and their unusual fatigue made a halt necessary. Word came that our artillery and ammunition wagons had mistaken their orders, which were to take a different and much longer road around the mountain, and had got as far up the hillside as the tired animals could draw their loads. The general sent Mc-Mahon and me back with directions to turn the batteries about and get them on their proper way. Now we could not ride down on the road, which was not much more than a footpath, and full of weary men lying where they had halted, so we started to go down the side of the mountain. My man Bennett rode a white horse that cast a faint glimmer a few steps off, so we let him go first, and took a zigzag direction down through the woods and over the rocks.

We got there somehow, stumbling and sliding, scratched and torn by the branches, and wet to the skin, and only the instinct of our good horses preserved us from going over some of the numerous precipices on the route. At the foot were the "red artillery," fast asleep in the narrow road. Every battery and wagon had to be harnessed and turned about by hand, and we had many fine opportunities to curb our tempers, for they did not like to be waked up and some were disposed to question our authority. At last, about three in the morning, the job was done, and finding a barn near by we led our worn-out horses into the haymow, and there we stretched out, master and man, upon the soft hay as upon a bed of Elysium. How good it felt! And

when Bennett produced a small flask of the wine
of the country, I believe even Neal Dow would
have joined us had he been in those parts. But
we could not sleep long. The farmer came out
to feed his cattle and discovered the three
tramps, and made us come in to breakfast. The
memory of those flapjacks is still regnant after
some thirty years. He and the goodwife may
have been gathered to their fathers long since,
and if living it is not probable they should ever
see these lines, but I wish they could know we are
still thankful.

The bright sun was shining, the meadows
were drying, as we cheerfully galloped along
through the beautiful valley to catch up with
our people, and it was restful not to be looking
out for guerrillas at every turn, as in Virginia.
We were getting down into a familiar country
again, lovely Maryland. As we came near the
pretty little village of Funkstown, a familiar
rattling skirmish fire made itself apparent, and
we could see in the distance a line of rebel infantry charging upon a thin and scattered blue
line of ours, and we saw the enemy give back
and run, then rally and come forward, only to
again break and go to the rear. The Vermont
brigade in a superb skirmish line were giving
their usual good account of themselves. Then
we caught up with our staff and were chaffed

vigorously upon our disheveled appearance. Two days and nights in the saddle would make even a young Adonis look unkempt. I had no claims to be an Adonis, but Andrews had, so when I rode with him into Funkstown, and saw a most beatific vision of a young woman, on the porch of the principal house, waving two Confederate flags, I noticed that her hostile eyes softened and she changed from a very Bellona to only a handsome girl, at the sight of my good-looking companion. Andrews said, "Let's call on the Funkstown traitress," and we did. She received us like a young queen, told of her rides of forty miles or more to carry intelligence to Stonewall Jackson, and gloried in her patriotism, while we gloried in her beauty. Before our duties called us beyond Funkstown, her hatred for the Yankees had relaxed and she was naught but "pure womanly." Where she is now I know not, but the prejudices of that day put one side, she was but a brave young American girl, — yes, a heroine.

Lee's army had got into position in a semicircle on our side of the Potomac, and we looked them over with a view of attacking. There was a council of war, and as usual we didn't fight. It has always been clear to my mind that the council was right. I had the presentiment often told that I was going to be killed that day, and I respected the decision of the council. It was a question of attacking intrenched works with no special advantage on our side. Such a thing was dangerous then ; in these later days of war, simply impossible. The blunder of letting them get and intrench the position should weigh heavily upon the reputation of the general who was responsible for it.

That night over the river they went in a most masterly way. Our cavalry picked up a lot of prisoners, and the next evening about a thousand were turned over to me to care for. Seeing a beautiful field, I corralled them there under guard and went to much-needed sleep, which was soon broken by a message that the general wanted to see me. He made apparent to my dazed senses that my field was within hail of the rebel pickets on the other side of the Potomac, and that my prisoners would before morning " silently steal away." It is unnecessary to say that I promptly removed them, but it is one of my many pleasant recollections of my kind general that this time his chaff was silent and he did not tell the boys.

CHAPTER XXVII.

"But ever a blight on their labors lay,
    And ever the quarry would vanish away."
                            RUDYARD KIPLING.

AGAIN the Army of the Potomac crossed its
natal river. Our corps brought up, after several marches, at the beautiful little town of
Warrenton, where we remained many weeks.
Our duties were light and festivities frequent.
Why we stayed so long during the fine fall
weather we did not know, but we could easily
be contented with our surroundings. It was
possible to go to the Warren Green Hotel and
sleep in a room if we chose. We had horse-
races, reviews, and many an evening serenade.
The general's old division of the 2d corps
presented him with a splendid horse and trap-
pings, and we entertained a thousand guests
that day. They came from all the corps of
the army, but our good cheer did not give out
or the fun abate till, at midnight, a quarter-
mile race by moonlight between the crack horses
of the corps, ridden by their owners, closed
the merry-making. The order kept in Warren-

ton and the security to property became so marked that at length the people received us at their houses in the most friendly manner. Afterward, the young ladies were taken to task by their friends in the Southern army for being polite to the hated Yankees, but General Lee told them "he knew Sedgwick well, and he would have no one about him it would not be safe to know." When we first came, however, the bitterness displayed by these same girls was well expressed by one of their favorite songs, running as follows : —

" You can never win us back ; never ! never !
   Though we perish in the track of your endeavor,
   Though our corpses strew the earth
   That smiled upon our birth,
   And blood pollutes each hearthstone forever !

" We have risen to a man, stern and fearless ;
   Of your curses and your taunts we are careless.
   Every hand is on its knife,
   Every gun is primed for strife,
   Every palm contains a life high and peerless.

" You have no such blood as ours for the shedding ;
   In veins of Cavaliers it had its heading ;
   You have no such stately men
   In your Abolition den,
   Who marched through death and danger, nothing dreading.

" Though we fall beneath the fire of your legions
   Paid with gold, — murd'rous hire ! base allegiance ! —
   For every drop you shed

We shall have a mound of dead,
And the vultures shall be fed in our regions!

" The battle to the strong it is not given
While the Judge of right and wrong is in heaven;
While the God of David still
Guides the people with His will,
There are giants yet to kill, wrongs unshriven!"

Beaumont, our poet laureate, soon sang it back in another version to his tuneful guitar: —

"Oh! yes, we'll win you back, rebel beauties,
With 'sugar and hard-tack' to your duties;
Even now you greatly prize the glance of Yankee eyes,
And, for lovers, Yankee soldiers well they'd suit ye's!

" Our camps are thronged with ladies and with lassies,
For Salem and White Plains seeking passes;
Every one desires a guard, and think it's mighty hard
If she can't get lots of sugar and molasses.

"No, we've no such men as yours for the showing,
Of 'Cavalier' descent always blowing;
On convicts' seedy scions transformed to Southern lions;
Forsooth, you have great cause for your crowing!

" The back-bone of the 'so-called' has been shattered,
And the hordes of the unholy have been scattered,
And you tremble lest the walls of Sumter on you fall,
By 'Monitors' and 'Swamp Angels' battered.

"'T would be hard to feed your vultures in these regions,
After having been traversed by your legions;
Every cussed thing to eat they stole on their retreat,
And there's nothing left but chestnuts and persimmons."

This laid the offensive ditty to rest, and the répertoire of the fair singers retained nothing

more partisan than " God Save the South," " The
Origin of the Harp," and like songs then in
fashion. I would be glad to have now the verses
written and sung in those idle days, for the associations they would recall. One chorus still lingers : —

> " McMahon sighs and damns the eyes
> Of every one who looks upon
> Fannette the fair, with golden hair,
> The loveliest maid in Warrenton."

About the middle of September we marched
to Stone House Mountain, and remained there
some three weeks, and then on to Culpeper,
coming in sight of Lee's army. We expected a
great battle for some days, and then marched
back to Centreville near Washington, Lee on
our flank, and each army watching a chance to
get the other at disadvantage. One day at Centreville, the rain coming down in sheets, a hatless
officer burst into our tent and said he had just escaped from Mosby, that Captain —— , who was
with him, had been taken, and that Mosby was
behind our lines. As I had scouted the country
well over the day before, I thought he would go
out by Frying Pan Shoals, so ordered a squadron
of Vermont cavalry, who were our provost guard,
to saddle up, and several of us went out with
them in hopes to cut him off. We rode some
fifteen miles at a rapid pace to the supposed out-

let, and got into ambush ; but too wet and cross to remain there patiently, we started back on the route we expected him to come out. I sent a sergeant ahead with orders to throw up his hand as soon as he heard anything on the road, we following at a trot with drawn and sharpened sabres, and under orders to use nothing else. After a couple of miles, the sergeant gave the signal, and we charged down the narrow and winding road as fast as good horses could go, expecting to meet and smash him by our impetus. Nothing appeared, however, and we wended our homeward way through the soaked and sodden woodlands with a disgust too deep for words. Some time after, the captured captain was exchanged, and his story was that Mosby was on this road with about a hundred of his people ; that they heard us first and went off by the left flank into a deep ravine ; and that he saw us through the underbrush go by on the gallop, but could not utter a sound as two pistols were held at his head, and that Mosby said it was Kilpatrick. I have often wondered who would have come out best had he charged us also. They would have been two to one, but we were far the " maddest."

I leave to the tactical historian the description of the grand tactics of the fall of '63. In process of time we neared Warrenton again. Be-

GENERAL D. A. RUSSELL

fore leaving there Kent and Andrews had put in charge of the young ladies two bottles of champagne, to be given to General J. E. B. Stuart, commanding the Confederate cavalry and their classmate at West Point, when he should come that way.

On our return we went in with our cavalry, and the rebel cavalry skirmished out as we came in. We proceeded at once to the friendly Virginia mansion; the fair ladies ushered us into the dining-room, and there were the champagne bottles and the heel taps in the glasses, where Stuart and his staff had been drinking the health of his old chums but a very few minutes before. There are few amenities in a civil war to record, but when Stuart died a soldier's death soon after, rather sadness than exultation was felt at 6th corps headquarters.

While in this camp, moved by the splendid success of the Vermont brigade, kept in full ranks by the pride of their State, I made a strong effort to have a Maine brigade formed and attached to the corps. Generals Sedgwick and Meade approved the idea cordially, and it was intended to take the 5th, 6th, and 7th Maine, already in the corps, to join them to the 29th, General Beal, and the 30th, General Fessenden, just ready to leave the State. The plan went well till it reached General Halleck, the marplot of the war, and he "sat on it," giving no reason.

November 7th we were ordered out of camp and left our luxurious quarters without a sigh. It did not seem as if we had been earning our money for quite a while, and it was time to be putting down the rebellion again.

We moved toward Rappahannock Station, arriving there late in the afternoon, and found in our front a chain of strong forts heavily occupied by the foe. It was soon evident that we were to attack them, and attack them we did. It was almost dark when the double skirmish line moved forward, General D. A. Russell in command. I took an order to him as he was starting, already wounded, and every shot from the enemy was a jet of fire, while all was quiet and dark on our side. The forts were covered with spitting fireworks as our first line, the 6th Maine and 5th Wisconsin, went through the ditch and climbed the rampart. Then there was a hand to hand fight of fifteen minutes; Upton's brigade came in on the left, and the prizes of victory were eight guns, four flags, and two brigades of Stonewall Jackson's old division, prisoners.

The next morning I counted forty of the 6th Maine, great stalwart fellows, lying dead, close to each other. I was up all that night caring for the prisoners. I regaled the two brigade commanders with the best I had to eat and army whiskey galore, and an hour afterward when Colonel Scofield, our corps commissary, received them at his camp and offered refreshments, one of them answered, " Not one mouthful, sir, till my men are fed ! " I strolled among the prisoners and marked their angry looks, and though somewhat ragged, they were a fine hardy lot of soldiers, intensely mortified to have been taken behind works, by an attack of two brigades only.

CHAPTER XXVIII.

"And enterprises of great pith and moment
With this regard their currents turn awry,
And lose the name of action."

Hamlet.

W E went into what promised to be our winter camp near Rappahannock Station, and corps
headquarters were at the grand old Welford
mansion, now deserted. Its hospitable doors
must have been opened near a century, and have
ushered many a squire and dame of the olden
time to quaint revels and rich feasts. Perhaps
Braddock and his young aide-de-camp quaffed
there the loving cup on their way to Fort Du
Quesne ; perhaps Patrick Henry with his magic
tongue may have held spellbound his fellow-
patriots around its generous board. But no
greater honor had been bestowed upon its roof
in all its years of glory and prestige than that of
sheltering John Sedgwick during the last happy
months of his life. Nowhere do his young staff
officers recollect him better than here. A lion
in battle, but with the harness off, gentle as a
woman, unselfish as a saint. Surely those of us
who made his military family then can look back

upon no greater privilege, no more lasting recollection than being permitted to enjoy his confidence and appreciate his simple greatness.

We soon built ourselves houses, or fixed up our
tents comfortably with rough chimneys and fireplaces and board floors, and settled down to the
routine of winter quarters, as we supposed.
Many visitors from the North and the constant
demands of hospitality, entailed by the coming
and going of our many friends through the corps
and the army, filled the days very well. Some
English officers from Canada, among whom I remember General Earl, afterward killed in Egypt,
Lord Castlekuff and Captain Peel, a brother of
Sir Robert Peel, spent some time with us, and
many parties were given in their honor. We
used to illustrate the great politeness of one of our
number by telling how, after helping the young
sprig of nobility into the saddle, he said, " I beg
pardon, my Lord Castlekuff, I don't want to dis-
turb you, but your horse is standing on my foot."
The Englishmen bore themselves very well all
through the rest of the army only to come to grief
among the horse artillery.

The cold in Virginia when it does come is a
bitter, biting sort of cold, piercing to bone and
marrow, even though the temperature may not
be so low. The roads were all frozen solid, and
the powers above us thought it would be a good

scheme to cross the Rapidan, try to take Lee by surprise and beat him in detail before he could concentrate his army. The idea was good enough, but the carrying out of this Mine Run campaign, as I think about it now, reminds me of Kinglake's "Crimea," that tragedy of errors. As I remember it, we started out in fine spirits, and Whittier got off one of his famous puns. He wanted me to wait a minute for him, and as I demurred and galloped off, called out, " Time and T. Hyde [tide] wait for no man."

This frosty, bracing Thanksgiving morning reminded us of our beloved Northern winter. We were young and fond of change, but when we got to the river and found the 3d corps, who led our column, were not over because "some one had blundered, " gloom began to set in. Farrar, my chum, had had a bearskin bag made large enough for both of us to crawl into, with a flap to cover the entrance to the thing. We laughed at it at first, but I did not laugh the six or eight nights we were out, except from sheer comfort, as the others were trying to keep warm. We all got into bivouac, after midnight, and at dawn pulled out again, following the 3d corps. They very soon lost their way, for it was the Wilderness country, and one road or track in the dense thickets could not be distinguished from another : and after a while stumbled into John-

son's rebel division, who may have lost their way
also. This brought about a fight, and a sharp
one, too.

We came up close to support General French,
and while we were not much engaged at Locust
Grove, a more trying afternoon I never passed.
Most of the cannon-balls fired at the 3d corps
struck the frozen ground and bounced over into
us. We were sitting on our horses in a clearing
with nothing to do but watch these balls, which
could be seen like a swift-flying baseball, but
each sounded like the wail of a lost spirit. One
seemed to come directly for me. It could not be
dodged, but it swerved a little, and smashed to
pieces two innocent stretcher-bearers close by
who were carrying off a wounded man who was
insensible. As soon as he was dashed to the
ground, however, he rushed for the woods with
maniacal yells. This was very depressing.

Our people got the better of them at last,
and the next morning we took the lead and
fought our way till we were out of the Wilderness and could see Lee's army nicely concentrated in front on the hills beyond Mine Run.
Some one's mistake, a pontoon too short, and
a guide missing, had lost us all our good chances.
But the generals made their plans, and we were
kept riding everywhere, till late at night we
learned that our general was to make a storming

column of the 5th and 6th corps, some 30,000 men, go beyond our right and attack the enemy's flank at a certain signal next morning. We were all night at work getting into position in the sombre forests, and when, as morning dawned, I rode along the front of the column, there were our Maine regiments, the Vermonters, and the Regulars in the front line, and many bets were being made which would be in the enemy's intrenchments first. But what are the little white patches on all these overcoats of army-blue? For the first time I saw the men had pinned their names on their breasts, that their bodies might be recognized in the carnival of death they expected, but did not shun. That assault would have been a winner had it been delivered, I believed then, and believe now. Kent and I were ordered by the general to go in with the stormers, and, as it was not quite time for the signal, I hunted up corp headquarters, and found them at a negro house in a hollow. The boys and the English officers who had accompanied us had taken judicious shelter behind the great brick chimney which is always built outside at one end of these abodes of happiness. The enemy were flinging shells our way with great recklessness. MacCartney's men were pushing his guns by hand up over the rise, and firing one by one. The general was on the crest, leaning against a

tree, in full view of the rebels, looking at them
with his glass, and waiting for the signal to advance from far over to our left. MacCartney
and Colonel Tompkins were standing near him.
Then as we all happened to be looking, a round
shot cut the tree off as if with a knife, a foot
higher than the general's head, and we could all
testify that he did not even lower his spyglass.
We were not sorry the English officers were
looking, too.

But now a mounted officer dashes up, hands
a dispatch to the general, and we soon knew the
order to assault was countermanded. Warren, on
the left, had found the enemy too strong in his
judgment, had suspended his attack, which ours
was to follow, and so the whole grand plan was
futile. I cannot say I was personally very sorry.
The prospect of going over that run and up the
long slope and through the slashings with forty
cannon, to say nothing of musketry, playing our
way, and going mounted, too, had not been com-
mending itself to my imagination for some little
time. I did not mind going mounted so much,
for it is just as safe, and one can be more useful.
The only assault I ever went into dismounted,
I found myself at great disadvantage in commanding troops. We marched back to Welford's
again, cold and disgusted, and began a long winter's rest.

CHAPTER XXIX.

" And bright
The lamps shone o'er fair women and brave men ;
A thousand hearts beat happily ; and when
Music arose with its voluptuous swell,
Soft eyes looked love to eyes which spake again,
And all went merry as a marriage-bell."

BYRON.

THERE was something fascinating about our winter city of 100,000 men. Sheltered by huts and tents, warmed by huge wood fires, wakened by blare of bugle and tap of drum, sleeping often to dream of our dangerous and uncertain future, mingled with visions of glory, too, the young soldiers of the Republic, with a confidence in the final success of our cause scarcely felt at the North, passed their time in such amusements as they could invent. Reviews, balls, races, and the mail from home were the joyful incidents that dispelled monotony. An occasional trip to Washington, that muddy Mecca, a ten days' leave for home, where we could pose for heroes to our hearts' content, made the time all too short. Most of us knew nothing of business not military, and little of politics, and " to ride, to shoot, and to speak the truth " nearly filled the circle of our acquirements, as in the days of Cyrus the Great. One corps after another gave a ball to all the rest of us, and, as many officers had their wives or sisters in camp, there was a sprinkling of feminine loveliness among the many hundreds of blue uniforms, and if a man got a partner of the other sex once in an evening he thought himself lucky. The improvised ballrooms were vast, the bands of music large and good, and the refreshments most profuse, but the male wall-flowers were, alas, in a large majority.

The general was good enough to have some of his young lady relatives and friends down for a visit. We gave up our best quarters and did what could be done for their entertainment. All our resources were compelled to do them homage. One of their number, as daring and graceful an equestrienne as any Virginia, fair land of horsewomen, could boast, accompanied me across Hazel River and beyond our farthest pickets. We galloped on toward the sun, just setting behind the distant Blue Ridge, scarcely recking that hostile people might be abroad, till prudence called a halt and bade a swift return.

As spring approached, the army daily became larger from fresh enlistments and the return of those who had been wounded or exchanged from prison. Rumor told us that General Grant was coming to take command. As we had sad experience of a Western general with his headquarters in the saddle, we were half inclined not to like it much; but the record and Lincoln's opinion were in his favor, and when it became understood that he was to have his own way without interference from Washington, we determined to let our opinions of him be governed by the events to come. While never very enthusiastic over Grant, the Army of the Potomac forgave the cruel and unnecessary losses they sustained under him on account of the results attained. It was not that enthusiasm had died out among us, for Sheridan could rouse plenty of it afterward, but we had exhausted much of our early fervor, and envied the Confederates their great captain.

Then, too, we thought people North hardly comprehended that the Army of the Potomac had been fighting the choicest leadership and the best army by far of the Confederacy, and all the time with a rope around its neck tied to the doors of the war department. But Grant came, and brought the little fellow with him named Sheridan to command the cavalry, and we began to think that perhaps they would do the business after all. They reviewed us, corps after corps, and emulation as to who would make the best appearance ran high. General Torbert of the New Jersey brigade was a very handsome

man and the best-dressed officer in the army.
He had magnificent horses, a saddle which was
said to have cost five hundred dollars, with
accoutrements to match, and when he passed a
reviewing stand it usually caused a sensation.
As our corps passed General Grant, from our
proper places, we watched him carefully for some
expression or mark of approval, but so far as we
could see he did not seem even to be thinking.

After we got back to camp and had dismounted, Whittier asked, " What did General
Grant think of us ? What did he say, General ?
He made one remark to you." " He said Torbert rode a good horse," replied the general, as
he sought the interior of his tent and his ever-
lasting game of " solitaire." We would like to
know the exact words of Napoleon or Wellington
on any occasion, and posterity may want to know
likewise the words of Grant, the taciturn, and it
is certain that to others than his very intimates
they were few in number.

As April (1864) passed away, rumor almost
daily announced an advance preliminary to the
mighty wrestle that must take place between the
two great armies: ours much the larger, but still
hardly equal to the Confederates when making
the attack, on account of the rough, tangled,
wild, and densely wooded country, like none in
which civilized warfare was ever before waged,
well named the Wilderness.

CHAPTER XXX.

"Better like Hector in the field to die
Than like a perfumed Paris turn and fly."
                                    LONGFELLOW.

MAY 4, 1864, we were up at 2.30 A. M., and
soon on our way again to cross the Rapidan.
These early awakenings were usually completed
by my servant pouring a couple of canteens of
water on my head, followed by a brisk rub, and
a dipper of black coffee. This satisfactory stim-
ulant and a hard-tack to gnaw carried one along,
albeit in a savage frame of mind, till a halt at
seven or eight o'clock for breakfast. The birds
were singing, the fruit trees were blossoming,
and the scent of spring was in the air. Before
night we were over the pontoon bridges and in
bivouac three miles south of the river.

At daybreak, the corps was pushed out slowly
on a narrow road to the right, and we found we
were to form the right of the army. Firing was
soon heard to our left, where the 5th corps
were known to be. I rode with General Sedgwick to Meade's headquarters, which were near
the ruins of a mill on the main road, running
south. After a while Meade said, "Sedgwick, I

am short of staff officers. Will you lend me
one?" The general beckoned to me, and General Meade said, "Go back to Germania Ford,
and you will meet General Grant coming to
the front. Tell him Lee is moving down the
plankroad and the turnpike, and I have pushed
Warren and the 6th corps out to meet him."
I rode back as fast as possible on a road full
of troops.

When I had gone some four miles, I saw a
long cavalcade on the road and soon met General
Grant at its head. Saluting, I gave my message
verbatim, and fell in behind with Porter and
Babcock. The pace was soon accelerated, and
when we got to Meade's headquarters, I kept as
near as possible to hear what would be said.
General Grant dismounted, and General Meade
came forward on foot to meet him, and I heard
him tell him just about the same as I had,
nothing new having transpired. Grant said,
"That is all right," and sat down under a tree,
lit a cigar, and began to whittle. The firing
now became hotter. I was sent with an order
to General Burnside, and on my return General
Meade told me to go to General Ricketts, commanding our 3d division, and to put him in line,
in what position I have now forgotten. On
getting to Ricketts, I gave him the order and
found General Dent, of Grant's staff, had just

given him an order to go to another place. This
puzzled Ricketts, but I told him he had better
obey Meade's order as the last one given, and
dashed back to see if I was right. General
Meade said, " You did just right, sir, but go back
as soon as possible and tell General Ricketts to
obey General Grant's order."

These words made an indelible impression in
my memory, and show that Grant, while leaving
the command practically in Meade's hands during this campaign, did sometimes interfere in details. After remaining with Meade four or five
hours, riding some thirty miles and tiring out two
horses, I was released and got back to the general
to find the line of the 6th corps busily engaged at
close quarters with the unseen enemy. The staff
were at a cross-roads. The enemy had two or
three guns up, but we had none on account of the
dense forest. They seemed to have our range,
and several good horses had been knocked out
already. Then a shell burst under the horses of
two war correspondents, — Jerome D. Stillson
of the " World " was one, — and they were advised to go to the rear. The firing redoubled in
front, the Jersey brigade was double-quicking by
us to reinforce the line, and I had dismounted to
fix my horse's bit, when a cannon-ball took off
the head of a Jerseyman ; the head struck me,
and I was knocked down, covered with brains

and blood. Even my mouth, probably gaping in
wonder where that shell would strike, was filled,
and everybody thought it was all over with me.
I looked up and saw the general give me a sor-
rowful glance, two or three friends dismounted
to pick me up, when I found I could get up myself, but I was not much use as a staff officer
for fully fifteen minutes.

The afternoon passed in a succession of charges
and counter-charges. The shrill rebel yell alter-
nated with the deep hurrah of our people, and
neither side gained much, though we got a few
hundred prisoners. Among them was an officer
of the 18th Mississippi who had been in my
hands twice before. After dark I was sent with
a message to General Seymour, commanding our
right brigade, and as they were firing it was easy
to get there, but only on foot. To get back was
another matter. There was nothing to guide one
in the bushy, briery labyrinth. Sense of direction I had none, and so wandered about till morning, sometimes fancying I had strayed into the
enemy's lines, and lying quiet till I could catch
the accent of those talking. I heard none of the
Southern dialects, however, and wet, torn by
thorns, and hatless, by daybreak I found my comrades, still wearily sleeping by the roadside, holding their horses, with their saddles for pillows.

The firing began as soon as light, and the

scenes of the day before were repeated. Occasionally tremendous crashes of musketry off to the left announced that the other corps were at it. News kept coming of the terrible losses of part of our 2d division, which had been sent under Getty to reinforce the 2d corps. The general was exceedingly anxious about his right, and near noon sent me scouting to the river and back to see if there were any signs of the enemy getting around us. I saw nothing and returned safely. A few years ago, General Gordon, who commanded opposite, told me that about the same time with a courier he did the same thing, and came in behind our right, but was not discovered. He saw enough of our position, however, to lead his subsequent attack skillfully. Our 3d division, which had recently joined the corps, had the right of our line, and about five o'clock Gordon struck them square on the flank. They crumbled up, and our first intimation of it was throngs of excited men pushing through the bushes for the rear. The general sent part of us off to the right to rally them, and went straight down the road himself, wherever he went holding his line by his personality. Arthur McClellan and Captain Hayden succeeded with me in getting several hundred men together in a clearing, and were pushing them forward in a tolerable line with several colors, when a brigadier-general, in full uniform, burst out of the woods and frantically ordered them to halt, and at the same moment Gordon's troops struck us. Our line, having lost momentum, disintegrated at once. Had they been in motion, I think they would have kept on. Hayden was shot through both his legs, McClellan's horse was killed, and I threw myself between my horse's neck and the fire and barely escaped capture. Soon I met a colonel, mounted, whose face bore the most abject expression of terror I ever witnessed. I asked him if our line held. He said, " It was all gone." I asked where were the 7th Maine. He answered they were wiped out. This was pretty bitter news, and I took the direction from which he had come, with the idea of verifying it or sharing their fate, but I only succeeded in running the gauntlet of Gordon's fire again. Then I got back to the main road. I found many guns in position, and Crawford and the Pennsylvania reserves marching up, having been sent us by Grant as a reinforcement. I told Crawford where he had better put his troops, and then went to the 5th corps line, and down it to ours, which had stood like a rock, and on to the 7th Maine holding its extreme right, refused. To my joy I found the regiment had changed front to rear on the 10th company, and with the 43d New York had stopped

the rout, but at a great cost; about half were
killed and wounded, and the colonel, lieutenant-colonel, and major of the 43d had
been killed near our colors. But there was
brief time for condolence, and grief must be indulged later. I soon found the general, and
under his guidance, with a couple of lanterns,
Kent and I spent the night running out a new
line for the corps. This was almost perpendicular to our old line, and before morning we had
the troops on it. Just after light we met the
Vermonters, who had returned from their desperate fighting under Hancock, who, as soon as
they saw the general, broke out into wild cheering. He blushed like a girl as he saluted their
colors, and it seemed to go far to compensate
him for the mortification of the mishap of the
evening before.

All the day we kept our line waiting for attack, which did not come. About noon, after I
had snatched a little sleep, I was sent off with a
squadron of cavalry to our front with orders to
find out if they were making any movement to
get between us and the river. After coming to
a little hamlet, whose name I have forgotten,
but there were signs of ancient iron manufacture
about it, and hearing firing beyond, I left most
of my horsemen, and with a few went toward
the noise. Posting what men I had at each

cross-road for warning should any enemy appear, I finally found myself in rear of a rebel skirmish line engaged with our people, and I could see from the general direction of the fire that the action was not resultant from any move to get around our right. Thinking their line of battle might advance and catch me, I swiftly withdrew, picked up my cavalry, and reported results. I saw that day a colored division for the first time. They had been marched about a good deal, what for, it was hard to tell. They were actually white with dust, and as I passed, a big sergeant was prodding those he could reach with the butt of his gun, and saying, " Clos' up dere, lambs."

By night orders came to go southward. Though we had had as much fighting as we wanted, this was better than crossing back over the Rapidan, which rumors of disaster after disaster seemed to indicate. Never did a night's march seem harder. Having been for three days and two nights on a constant nervous strain, and with scarcely any sleep, this night was a medley of phantasmagoria. Positively light-headed as well as ragged and dirty, hungry and thirsty, I ran into Charley Whittemore's quarter-master's camp in the morning and found for a brief time comparative luxury and then repose. There was coffee and broiled chicken, and a chance to wash, as well as a royal welcome. Charley has joined the silent majority, but his happy disposition and kind heart remain as a pleasant memory to his surviving friends.

To say we were glad to be out of the Wilderness is putting it mildly. We left there and in the jolting ambulances near 20,000 of our best and bravest.

CHAPTER XXXI.

"Well indeed might they be shaken
By the weight of such a blow:
He has gone, their prince, their idol,
Whom they loved and worshiped so."

AYTOUN.

Down the turnpike road to Spottsylvania on the morning of the 8th of May tramped the diminished and dusty column of the 6th corps. At its head, as usual, General Sedgwick's stalwart form, but his face was saddened by our losses, and possibly by a foreboding of the fate he rode so gravely to meet. In the afternoon we caught up with the once distant firing, came to dead men by the roadside, met the usual pale and bloody victims upon stretchers, and soon General Robinson, commanding the division of the 5th corps that were engaged, minus one of his legs. Lee was in front of us and intrenching fast, so our tired troops were got forward into line as soon as possible.

The dim impression of that afternoon is of things going wrong, and of the general exposing himself uselessly and keeping us back, of Grant's coming up and taking a look, of much bloodshed and futility. Then the dismal night in the tangled forest, the hooting of owls, the embrace of the wood-tick, bang-bang from the picket line, then a dozen more, then the dreamless repose of utter fatigue.   The fiat of " Fight it out on this line if it takes all summer " had been pronounced, and as most of us did not think much of this line discouragement began to set in.   We did not then appreciate the policy of attrition, and thought our lives as good as the rebels', man for man.

On the morning of the 9th, the corps seemed to be in a fairly good position ; headquarters were near a cross-road where a dropping fire of sharp-shooters was making sad havoc with anything of ours in sight.   General Morris and Colonel Locke had already been carried to the rear.   The general sent me to advance our pickets a little, I suppose to rid us of this annoyance.   I rode down to them through an open field, taking a zigzag course as fast as my good horse could run, which no doubt saved me, as little spurts of smoke kept bursting from the distant woods, and the unpleasant whistle of rifle bullets was very apparent.

My errand done, I got back in the same way, and sat down beside the general on the ground. He was sitting on a cracker box behind a tree, and began pulling my ears affectionately, and chaffing me a little as I was trying to fill my

COLONEL M. T. MC MAHON

pipe, and to tell him about my ride. Then a
section of artillery came up the road at the trot
and went to the right into position. He got up
and went over to give them some directions, I
thought. Directly I heard some one cry out,
" The general; " and hastening over there, saw
lying on his back, our friend, our idol. Blood
was oozing slowly from a small wound under
his eye. McMahon was trying to raise him up.
Tompkins, Beaumont, Whittier, Halsted, and
others of the staff gathered mournfully around;
the men had risen upon their knees all along the
line and were looking on in sorrow. Gradually
it dawned upon us that the great leader, the
cherished friend, he that had been more than a
father to us all, would no more lead the Greek
Cross of the 6th corps in the very front of
battle; that his noble heart was stilled at last!
Our personal loss was then paramount, but
many through the army said Meade could have
better spared his best division. We bore him
tenderly to an ambulance, and followed it to
army headquarters where an evergreen bower
had been prepared, and there he lay in simple
state with the stars and stripes around him.
All who came remained to weep; old grizzled
generals, his comrades for many years; young
staff officers, and private soldiers: all paid this
tribute to his modest greatness. Three of the

staff accompanied the remains to Cornwall Hollow, Conn., his birthplace and home. The lines that follow express somewhat the sympathy between Sedgwick and his command; their authorship is unknown: —

TO SEDGWICK — IN MEMORIAM.

A little valley fenced by natural walls,
Through which a brook winds toward the neighboring
     river;
A little graveyard where the sunlight falls
On green mounds over which no willows shiver;
Nor leaves of pine, on the mountain's head,
Keep the wild snowdrift from their peaceful bed;

A spot beloved by all the country folk —
Here Sedgwick lived, and here, by many a token
Of look and word and smile and homely joke,
They kept his image in their hearts unbroken;
Though few his visits now to that old home
Whose doors afar invited all to come.

Chief of the Sixth Corps!   In that silent home
One gentle spirit haunting it there lingers;
Her eye kindles and her thoughts arouse
At midnight dreaming of thee, and her fingers
Grasp the brief telegrams that thrill the world
Whene'er the Sixth Corps' banner is unfurled.

The clouds wept that morning when we met
At the dear mansion house in Cornwall Hollow;
We said but little, though our cheeks were wet
With the proud tears that evermore will follow
The hearse that carries home the noble dead;
And here we laid thee in this lowly bed.

Let the dust sleep among its kindred dust!
Father and mother, loving friend and neighbor;
And let the mountain pine, true to its trust,
Even like the hero, buffet and belabor
The wintry blast upon the distant hill:
Forever hallowed be that spot and still!

Yet he sleeps not there; for soul like his
Sleeps never after death.   At once it enters
Into the living forms of all that is;
Haunting the ages, lighting up the centres
Of crumbling states, of waning, wasting creeds,
And touching dead shapes with living deeds.

We bid thee farewell!   Cold as we are
We welcome thee in all familiar places;
We see thee in the eagle or the star;
And hail thee in a thousand happy faces
That smile upon our flag — on land or sea,
The symbol yet of faith and type of thee.

CHAPTER XXXII.

"They fell devoted, but undying;
    The very gale their names seemed sighing;
    The waters murmured of their name;
    The woods were peopled with their fame;
    Their spirits wrapt the dusky mountain;
    Their memory sparkled in the fountain;
    The meanest rill, the mightiest river,
    Rolled mingling with their fame forever."

Siege of Corinth.

WHEN one has been present at a dreadful and
sinister event, and has at the same time met a
grievous loss, the springs of life are loosened for
a while, and even the brightness of the world
is indescribably dreary. Till the elasticity of
youth resumed its sway, the rain-sodden woods of
Virginia seemed to cover but pathways where
all hope was lost. General Wright, since the
accomplished chief engineer of the army, assumed
command of the corps, and announced to us all
that we should retain our places. The evening
of the fatal 9th of May was spent in organizing
an attack of twelve picked regiments to take
place at dawn the next morning, and to be commanded by Colonel Emery Upton, ambitious to
gain his star.

My regiment, the 7th Maine, was one of

the chosen, and I coaxed McMahon, chief of staff, to substitute another. They never knew it, and since I have not been quite certain if I did right. It seemed to me they had lost so cruelly, but I certainly should not have liked it had I been the colonel and longing for advancement.

The morning of the 10th dawned wet and pale, and, as soon as it was light enough to see, away went the twelve regiments at the double-quick, through the woods with a rousing cheer, and poured over the enemy's breastworks, capturing several guns and a thousand prisoners. There they hung for a long time, unable to take the second line, and waiting for the support they had every reason to expect; it did not come. Then they were obliged to retire, but in good order, and with honor saved. At Marye's Heights and Rappahannock Station similar gallant charges were strongly supported, and why was it not so here? It is bootless now to inquire, but how it would have hurt our dead chieftain! The afternoon passed in skirmishing and artillery fire, and that night seven of our pickets were brought in from the line, crazy from want of sleep, and, as they were kept awhile by a camp fire before being sent to the rear, the scene was mournfully pathetic.

The next day was comparatively uneventful.

Rutzer, our headquarters purveyor, got up with some canned goods, and our appetites, which survived all misfortunes, were appeased for a time. That evening we got word that Hancock was to assault the works at Spottsylvania Court House, on our left, and that we were to be ready to support him. Little could we realize as we wrapped ourselves in our blankets, to dream of home, that the morrow was to bring the bloodiest battle ever fought on this continent. Before dawn we rose, and as the first gray light displayed a world of mist, the rattling volleys directed on the 2d corps began, and ours began the march toward them some few miles away. The whole corps moved out, and the general left me in charge of eighteen of our guns, which were directed to fire steadily at the enemy opposite. They were entirely without support. Here for some time I remained, speculating what the varying sounds of battle meant, and soon learning that Hancock had been successful, that he had taken Johnson's division prisoners with twenty guns, and that our people were engaged. This was delightful. But what if they should attack us here? was my anxious thought. By nine o'clock, however, a lot of heavy artillery regiments came up, and Arthur McClellan galloped to release me, and to tell of fighting that, even to his large experience, was terrific. Now to the corps with all speed, and, as they appeared through the ragged woods, I saw in the smoke the gallant New Jersey brigade reduced to a frazzle, with their colors close together. Sight and sound faded; I was on the ground, my orderly and his horse dead beside me, and as sense returned, I was mounted and away. My horse had stepped in a hole and thrown me over his head, but the sensation of death was not far absent.

On reaching headquarters, which were in a hollow a little behind the line, I found we were trying to hold part of the log breastworks Hancock had taken, against desperate efforts of large forces of Lee's army. Indeed, in a distance of less than a mile, the bulk of both armies were hurled at each other for twenty-two hours. General Wright sent me to General Meade to say that we must have reinforcements, that the corps could not hold much longer. It was like a running race to army headquarters, and when I got no satisfaction from General Meade it seemed to my excitement that I was responsible for it all. On returning, I came upon General Humphreys on the road, and told him my trouble. Said he, " Do you see that column of troops moving over there? That is Kitchen's brigade of heavy artillery; take him to support General Wright." The authority of the chief of staff of the army

was good enough for me, so I took Kitchen to
our corps line, where he soon lost his leg and a
large part of his command.   After the war, on
meeting General Humphreys, when, as chief of
engineers of the army, he was inspecting the
forts on the Maine coast, I asked him how it
was that I could get reinforcements from him
when the commanding general would give me
none, and he told me General Meade was suffering terribly that day from nervous dyspepsia
and had put him in charge.   ✓

So the day wore on apace.   Its memories are
of bloodshed surpassing all former experiences,
a desperation in the struggle never before witnessed, of mad rushes, and of as sudden repulses,
of guns raised in the air with the butts up and
fired over log walls, of our flags in shreds, and
at the short intervals which show what small
regiments are left.   It fell to my lot to order a
section of artillery into battery to assist our
musketry with canister.   I sent them, as ordered,
over a crest, but they did not seem to fire, though
it was little remarked in the pandemonium of
sound.   Soon night fell, but the next morning
when I saw them again they had not got into
battery.   Each piece and caisson were wheeled
half round, and every man and horse were there,
and they lay as if waiting the resurrection.

The night was dark and rainy, but the struggle did not abate. About nine o'clock General Wright told me to find General Griffin of the 5th corps, and tell him to come in in support, or our line must soon give way. But to find Griffin was another matter. For an hour or two I rode till I became completely lost. The only light was the firing and the dull glimmer of the faces of the dead. Feeling that the fate of all depended on me, I was wrought almost to madness, and to get my senses again I dismounted and sat down on the ground a while, holding my horse's bridle and my aching head till reason resumed its sway. Accident brought me to General Griffin at last, but he refused to obey, not being under General Wright's orders. He was technically all right, and as the corps still held on, no harm came of it. At two in the morning, after twenty-two hours of fighting, the enemy withdrew, and we all couched in the mud where we were, to wait for daylight.

I never expect to be fully believed when I tell what I saw of the horrors of Spottsylvania, because I should be loth to believe it myself, were the case reversed. The large tree trunk now in the war department cut off by musket balls bears witness to the intensity and continuance of the fire. Early next morning we went to visit the scene of the fighting. The breastworks were of heavy logs, and they had traverses, that is, other short breastworks perpendicular to them to protect from a flanking fire. The rebels were mostly between these traverses, and they lay two, three, and sometimes four tiers deep, the lowest tier nearly covered by blood and water. The wounded were often writhing under two or three of the dead. I undertook to relieve a young officer, who was nearly gone, of the weight pressed upon him, but he said ; shaking his head, " You have conquered ; now I die ; " and suited the action to the word.

Nor was the scene where lay the boys in blue less cruel. They were mostly in the open, — many nothing but a lump of meat or clot of gore where countless bullets from both armies had torn them ; all ploughed with many wounds, but each by himself on the greensward, lying in his last line of battle. Further on, where our people held the traverses, the same sickening scenes ; and the survivors, inured to all war's horrors, found new horrors there !

CHAPTER XXXIII.

" Join the cavalry."

Army Song.

LEE held upon Spottsylvania with a grip that no efforts of ours could unloosen. It had become a veritable woodland fortress. His lines were tried at every point from the 13th to the 18th of May. On the 14th, during an attempt to flank his right wing, Upton's brigade was sent forward from the Beverly House to occupy a clearing on a distant hillside that promised to be a good position, and I was sent with him. A venerable native went along as guide, and hardly had we debouched from the winding and rocky ascent when a rebel division charged us.

Our old guide was the first to fall, but there was no time to be horrified at his white hair streaked with blood. We were broken before having a fair chance to form. The 5th Maine fought its way over to the left and got off with little loss. I followed them in the falling darkness, and hearing rapid vociferation from a neighboring thicket, I discovered a sergeant with both legs shattered, and crazy from a wound in the head. He fancied he was in a class-meeting at home, and was preaching to an imaginary congregation at the top of his lungs, while the "whip-poor-will's complaint" could be heard from the neighboring grove. The pathetic mournfulness of it all followed me long.

In these days the Yankee soldiers went grimly to their doom in every charge, and the inner voice of the army was, "How long, O Lord, how long!"

On the 18th of May we made a bloody and unsuccessful attack, but were unable to pierce the broad tree slashings that surrounded the enemy. A little before this, Lieutenant Frank Glazier of my regiment had an enormous swelling come on his neck that resembled the goitre, but no one knew what it was. I saw him come out of this fight bleeding like a pig from a gunshot wound through this swelling; but the next day it had disappeared, leaving but an ordinary scar behind, and Frank as rugged and cheerful as ever. Arthur McClellan's bay horse had a shell pass directly through him as I happened to be looking. The distressing cry seemed to tear our ears, while the collapse of the beautiful animal was a picture of pain framed by the smoking forest.

Now another flanking movement gave a respite and a hope, and our shattered columns streamed out to the left toward the South Anna River.

While on the march, word came that a party of
the enemy's cavalry were on our flank. We had
with us some hundreds of convalescent men from
the cavalry corps who could not join their commands, as Sheridan was far away somewhere
fighting. Most of them were armed with Henry
rifles, a new breech-loading sixteen-shooter. I
was directed to organize them as best I could and
go out to drive away this cavalry force. Accompanied by Lieutenant R. S. Mackenzie, just from
West Point, who had a kind of a map of the
country, I tasted the joys of an independent cavalry command for the first time. With the regulation reserve on the road and with skirmishers
thickly deployed in front, on arriving at Massaponax church, we received a few harmless shots
and all hands began to fire back. I could soon
see that the Johnnies had not stopped upon the
order of their going, and had left a few dead
horses behind. Then for a long time we rode
back and forth behind our line trying to stop our
firing. It was no use. The rattling volleys continued till the ammunition was all gone, and General Wright, supposing us heavily engaged, sent
out a brigade and a battery to our assistance.
It was some time before I heard the last of the
" battle of Massaponax church," but it was quite
a lesson on the improper use of rapid-firing arms.
That brilliant soldier, and in later years renowned

Indian fighter, General Mackenzie, here received his baptism of fire, and then began between us a friendship that grew always warmer, till his inscrutable fate found him. The next day I was sent out again, and this time we had better luck. When we came upon the Confederate cavalry, they were posted on a good rise of ground by some farm buildings and evidently intended to stay there. I sent about a hundred mounted men around through the woods to where their flank ought to be with orders to charge and cheer when they struck it, and we would do likewise as soon as their noise was heard. These simple tactics worked to a charm. As soon as carbines commenced to crack over in the open woods to the left and front, we rushed them and ran them about two miles, till they got across some river, the Po, I think, and their friends on the other side began to throw canister at us. Then, loaded with spoils, bacon, chickens, and other good things to eat, we returned to camp, and I sighed to think I had not joined the cavalry in the beginning.

I will not attempt to recount the numerous conflicts that we took part in during the march southward. I would rather speak of lazy intervals, exploring ancient Virginia mansions, built when feudal magnificence held sway in these fertile valleys, and now left by their owners in care of faithful slaves alone. We found an ice house on every plantation now. While riding over a hot, dusty plain not far from Hanover Junction, I saw a man walking by a wagon train far in front, and said to myself, "If I did not know he was in Bath I should say that was the Rev. Dr. Fiske." On getting nearer it proved to be Dr. Fiske, who had come out to do what good he could, and the train belonged to the Christian Commission. He was ill, footsore, and weary, and had been doing his own cooking. I mounted him on my orderly's horse, and soon the best our headquarters offered was none too good for him. While with us he chanced to get under fire and saw men killed near him, and his coolness and courage were very much admired. Had he chanced to adopt the military profession instead of the church militant, I have never doubted that this delicate and refined clergyman would have made a great soldier.

CHAPTER XXXIV.

"Swift to be hurled —
Anywhere, anywhere,
Out of the world."

HOOD.

" Deep into that darkness peering
Long I stood there, wondering, fearing."

POE.

AFTER we got to Hanover Junction, where the
rebels managed to capture our efficient headquarters quartermaster, Platt, with many greenbacks in his possession, I was sent forward to
communicate our presence and advance to General Sheridan, fighting hard at Cold Harbor, to
hold it till the army came up. I had seen him before, but not to speak to him, and I found him the
most nervy, wiry incarnation of business, and
business only, I had yet met. Two of his divisions were fighting, dismounted, and seemed very
much like infantry except for their short jackets
and carbines. We had a belief in the infantry
that those carbines would not hit anything, and I
confirmed the belief so far as I was concerned by
borrowing one from a wounded man and firing in
the line for half an hour. To be sure there was
nothing but smoke to fire at as a general thing,
and though in dead earnest then, I am happy in

the conviction that I did not hurt anybody. By
and by the head of the 6th corps came up and
relieved the cavalry that night, getting into line
of battle and digging rifle pits all along the line
before sleeping.

The next day the Army of the Potomac was all
in position in front of the line of intrenchments
many miles long, held by Lee, near the old
battlefield of Gaines's Mills, where Porter and
the 5th corps so distinguished themselves. We
found an ice house where our quarters were
located, and entertained Grant and Meade and
their staffs; and many others were rescued for
a brief interval from the stifling heat and dust.
Among them my old friend, Dr. Mitchell, whom
I was very glad to see once more.

In the afternoon up came the 18th corps in a
tired column after a long march from Butler's
army. My old commander, "Baldy" Smith, was
at the head, and it seemed good to have his cool
and sagacious brain added to our leadership. Toward night we attacked in conjunction with the
18th corps, and while the attack generally spent
itself against breastworks in vain, some six hundred prisoners came in which my company of
cavalry promptly gathered and placed to the
credit of the 6th corps. The next morning I
heard General Smith was hunting after his prisoners, so I found him near his headquarters

wagon and told him I had them safe for him, as
I had ascertained they were mostly taken by the
18th corps. He was very much delighted and
treated his young subordinate as an equal for the
time we were together. On getting back to our
headquarters I found an enterprising photogra-
pher was taking a picture of them and the staff.
I got into line, and while the picture was being
taken, two mortar shells dropped behind our
tents. I have it now, and it is curious to see in
what rough and uncouth costumes, and in what
leanness of form and visage the whole party
stand forth. All were like athletes trained
down to the last limit for some great contest of
brawn and muscle. General Wright in the centre, with the corps flag above him; then Henry
Farrar, life of the camp and warm-hearted
friend; Charley Whittier, radiant in apparel,
and since a swell and a success in two con-
tinents; Halsted and Whittlesey, soon to cross
the dark river; Colonel Tompkins, chief of artillery, tall and handsome and of unrivaled excel-
lence in his profession; Kent, able soldier at all
points and exquisite gentleman as well; the laughing, plucky son of Oliver Wendell Holmes, now
an ornament to the bench; Arthur McClellan,
who knew no fear and against whom has never
been reproach; "Cub" Russell, cool and debo-
nair; Steve Manning, the reliable chief quarter-

Capt. Hayden   Capt. Holmes   Major Whittier   Col. Tompkins   Col. Franklin   Capt. Russell
Capt. Whittlesey   Capt. McClellan   Major Farrar   Major Tompkins   Col. Manning
Dr. Bland   Col. Hyde   Dr. Holman   Gen. H. G. Wright   Capt. Halsted   Col. Kent

SIXTH CORPS HEADQUARTERS AT COLD HARBOR

master ; and Walter Franklin, towering a head
above us in height, and in some other things too.
Several of the best and dearest of Sedgwick's
staff were absent, — McMahon, Pierce, Beaumont, and Andrews, — but we could not all be
off duty at once, even in a lull at Cold Harbor.

This battle was a series of attacks all along
the line, which was five or six miles long. Its
management would have shamed a cadet in his
first year at West Point. Seldom could we gain
a foothold anywhere even for a moment. Colonel James McMahon, brother of our chief of
staff, at the head of the Corcoran Legion, placed
his flag over their works, but his brother recognized him during a flag of truce the next day
only by his sleeve buttons. It is a maxim of
war that a direct attack against works held by
good troops can seldom, if ever, be successful,
and at Cold Harbor the attack was no heavier
at one place than another. That we lost 15,000
men and the enemy 1,500 is commentary enough
on the generalship of the commanding general
at this stage of his career.

While the burials were going on between the
lines during a flag of truce, nine rebel privates
strayed into our camps by mistake, were arrested
and sent to army headquarters. From there
they came under guard to the 6th corps with orders from General Meade to send them back at

once by flag of truce. When the order came to me to take them back, it was pitch dark. How to make a flag of truce visible I did not know, but the order was imperative, so I took them to our first division, General Russell's, which was lying in their fortified lines, a brigade in each line, and the lines connected by zigzag pits. Russell said there was no way to get them over, but I pushed on to the first line, the Jersey brigade under Penrose. They were lying down and firing as hard as they could at the enemy's pits in the dark some two hundred yards off, and the enemy were returning the fire with interest.

Indeed the same thing was going on for some three miles, and it would have been impossible for anything to live between those rows of breast-works. I asked Penrose to stop his fire and see if the rebels would not stop, and sure enough in a little while they did, only occasionally some fool would discharge his piece. At last I climbed over the works and stepped out into the unknown darkness beyond. Penrose came, too, and when we had groped some hundred yards I sung out, " I want to see the commander of the rebel line." " Say Confederate, for God's sake," said Penrose. I repeated my call, and it was answered quite near, " What do you want?" I told the reason of my coming, and they said, " Wait till we communicate with General Lee." Now there was nothing else to do but wait, and Penrose had gone back, and the thought came to me what it meant waiting there. If any irresponsible party fired his gun, it would all commence again just as it was going on to the right and left in vistas as far as I could see, and then there was no chance whatever for me. So I crouched in a half-filled grave and waited, despite the stench and horror of it all. It seemed hours before any one came, probably it was but a few minutes, and all the time black forms seemed to be encircling me in the blacker darkness. I could hear the low buzz from the rebel rifle pits close by, in the scarce intervals of the firing right and left. At last two of the black forms proved real, and were the colonel and his adjutant of a Mississippi regiment commanding the brigade just in front. I soon told my story, and, confident there would be no firing now, we sat down on the ground and exchanged supplies and stories for a time. Then I went back for my nine rebels, and we had to put them out by force over the rifle pits, they so dreaded the chance of the fire beginning. Right glad was I to see the last of them, as at two o'clock in the morning I wended my way through the zigzags to a dusty resting place beside the standard of the 6th corps. The roar of musketry was going on everywhere else as far as one could see, but Penrose's front was quite still, according to arrangement with the Mississippi colonel.

CHAPTER XXXV.

"They flee before our fierce attack!
    They fall! they spread in broken surges.
Now, comrades bear our wounded back,
    And leave the foeman to his dirges."
                                        STEDMAN.

IT is very interesting to revisit the battlefields
of the war, but I never heard any one who was
engaged there express a wish to see Cold Harbor again. Its vast upheavals of earth in fort
and rifle pit, in traverse and covered way, may
now have yielded to the sun, the rain, and the
plough, but it remains in memory the Golgotha
of American history. Gladly we turned our
backs upon it, and a day's march put us in
camp upon the banks of the beautiful James
River, where the evening was an idyl. The
luxurious vegetation, the scent of the flowers,
the fireflies' glimmer, with the sweet strains of
the Jersey band, made a welcome contrast to
our late surroundings.

The next day, while the corps was crossing
on the pontoon bridges, we boarded a "double-
ender" commanded by a brother of our Beaumont, and stared in envy at the white trousers
and fine uniforms of the officers. After receiv-

ing the usual hospitality of the navy, we were
given some blue regulation sailor shirts, and for
months I found them a most acceptable substitute for the army blouse. I remained for some
time after the corps had crossed with some cavalry to pick up stragglers, and after crossing the
river was sent to Bermuda Hundred, where part
of the corps had gone to support General Butler.
There was a fight threatening on his lines that
night, and it materialized to some extent, but the
only impressions of it left me are that General
Butler was very nervous, and that his headquarters were a long way from his line of battle. We
soon moved toward Petersburg, and our tents
were pitched again, after reposing in the wagons
for many weeks, on a good-sized hill which gave
a fine view of the rebel intrenchments, and the
distant spires of the city. I was awakened early
in the morning by a shell striking near, and got
out to find it had killed my orderly, who was
asleep in a shelter tent behind mine, and I saw
the tall form of Mr. Lincoln slowly walking away
to a more sheltered place. He had a long-tailed
black coat on and a rather battered high hat,
and he was leading his little son Tad by the
hand, occasionally looking back toward the rebel
batteries to see if another shot was coming.
But once again in life were the 6th corps destined to see him, and we realized this as little as

we then did that he was the great man of the century, beside whose all reputations are dim.

On June 21st we followed the 2d corps in a march to the left. The corps got into line on their left toward the Weldon Railroad, but there was no connection between the two corps. The next day was extremely hot, and there seemed to be a considerable force in our front. Firing began sharply on our right. Soon it ceased, and in twenty minutes broke out again a little nearer the centre, then shortly after about the centre. I had a theory, and wanted to test it, that the enemy were accustomed to do this till they could find our flank, or cavalry on it, for they could easily find them by the carbine fire; and here was the opportunity to prove my theory. I rode over beyond the left of our pickets where some cavalry were dismounted and thrown out in the woods as skirmishers, telling the officer in command of the picket as I went to look out for his left. Sitting on the piazza of a house and holding my horse's bridle, I listened to the picket fire for some time drawing nearer, and then stopping as if done on a regular plan. Suddenly it broke out in front, and I had barely time to get on my horse and escape before Mahone's division burst through the cavalry, took our pickets in reverse, and swept away a large portion of them as prisoners.

Not long ago I talked this over with General Mahone, and he told me it was a plan he had always used to find our flank.

As the 2d corps had met with a disaster, we were withdrawn and placed in the hottest and dustiest camp in which we had yet suffered. Some days after there came news of the defeat of Wilson's cavalry in a raid round the enemy, and we were ordered to Ream's Station to endeavor to extricate him. I was sent ahead of the column with a few hundred cavalry and a guide furnished by army headquarters. Knowing these scouts, or guides, often served both sides, while I rode ahead with him, deeply interested in his tales of adventure, I watched him narrowly, and when, as we stopped at a farm-house to get a drink, I detected a look of intelligence between him and the woman, I was very much on the alert.

At last in some open country we came upon a dozen rebel cavalry, and I halted for our cavalry to come up, but my guide kept on challenging me to charge them, and before I realized what he was about he had joined them and they all galloped off. Then we pushed on with the skirmishers in front, and, after a brief fight where they had obstructed the road, came out upon a plain, with Ream's Station and the railroad in the distance. Thinking there was nothing but cavalry holding the position, I got mine into line, dismounted, and advanced over some ploughed fields to receive a sharp fire from Finegan's Florida brigade in the railroad cut, which repulsed my attack. While I was trying to get them forward again, who should appear on the front line but my man Bennett, very red in the face, with a led horse, begging me to exchange my stallion for him, as he " feared Frank would get hurt. " As Bennett had a prejudice against musketry fire, his devotion was so much the more touching. Just as I got the cavalry on the advance again, to my delight I heard a ringing cheer behind, and, turning, saw the head of the corps, the Vermont brigade, double-quicking into line. Mr. Finegan heard them, too, and did not wait for them long, so we soon were in bivouac at the station as the dusk was falling. Two of us found a comfortable bunk in the pulpit of a church that night, though we were turned out several times by attacks on our pickets.

Wilson's raiders had got off some other way, so back went the corps to the dusty camp again. A few days after, I was ordered to Yellow Tavern on the Weldon Railroad with a battalion of New Jersey cavalry and orders to destroy as much of the road as possible. This regiment was called the " Butterflies " on account of their gaudy blue and yellow uniforms, and the battal-

ion reporting to me were all Germans. After a
march of some fifteen miles, we struck the railroad, and the men dismounted and went busily
to work bending the rails. The horses were left
in charge of each fourth man in a shady place
to the rear.

The destruction of a railroad was in those days
very simple. The iron rails were pried up and
put on fires of fence rails, where as soon as they
became hot enough they bent over at the ends by
their own weight. The "Butterflies" soon had
at least a mile of track torn up and many fires
started, when I thought I would climb up into
the attic of the old Yellow Tavern to see if any
of the enemy were visible. I had brought along
a dozen of our headquarters cavalry, the 1st
Vermont, and two of them followed me up to the
attic. Looking out of one of the two windows
I saw a mounted officer in a field beyond, and as
soon as the Vermonters saw him too, they began
cracking away with their carbines. The answer
was not slow in coming. Four guns were fired
by battery from the distant woods. One of the
shells came through that attic, disturbing the
dust of ages, so we had hard work to find our
way out. The other three burst over the led
horses, and when, half blinded, we got out of the
house, not a Dutchman was in sight. A cloud
of distant dust betokened the time they were

making.   My little squad of Vermonters had
dashed forward to a stone wall, and were engaging the now advancing enemy in a manner
delightful to witness.   On came the rebels,
very cautiously, and evidently thinking they had
to do with a large force.   After delaying them
as long as we could, at the right moment we ran
for our horses and dashed off, and when we had
got about six miles I met the German major, who
had succeeded in rallying quite a portion of his
" Butterflies," and they seemed very well satis-
fied with their performance.   Their excuse was
that the shells stampeded their horses and they
all went after them.   We had many kinds of
material in the Army of the Potomac and use
for most of it, but not for the " Uhlanen."

CHAPTER XXXVI.

"In the beauty of the lilies
Christ was born across the sea,
With a glory in his bosom that transfigures you and me:
As he died to make men holy, let us die to make men free,
While God is marching on."

JULIA WARD HOWE.

ORDERS came for us to march to City Point and take shipping. For once the all-knowing staff were at fault. We could not tell where we were going. Some had it to take Wilmington, some that riots had broken out in New York, and some that we were to join the Western Army; but no one knew that one Jubal Early was on the warpath in Maryland with his corps of seasoned veterans, and that the 6th corps was pulling up its shelter tents to get on his trail. Out of the dust, out of the heat, away from infinite winged insects, and then the clean side-wheelers received us for a day and a night, rolling on the summer sea. Vigor came with the breath of salt air, hope rose high in youthful hearts, almost numbed into insensibility by the long carnage which had swept away more than a third of the Army of the Potomac since Grant's banner crossed the Rappahannock at Germania

Ford.   The morning saw us passing Mount Ver-
non ; the loom of the great city and fortress was
in the distance, and, still unconscious of what
fate had in store for us, we landed our first brigade on the ruined wharves of Washington.

Cannon were booming out toward Tenallytown ; artillery practice, said we, but the closed
stores and the concourse of carts and people
moving off merchandise soon apprised us that
the foe was near.   Starting the first brigade at
speed toward the firing, General Wright and
staff galloped in hot haste toward Halleck's headquarters for orders and information.   The heat
was appalling, the orders vague enough, and the
information of all kinds.   But under the banners of the Greek Cross was disembarking a ragged and bronzed lot of soldiers in very business-
like haste, and soon a sturdy column of twelve
thousand veterans was going up the avenue and
out Seventh Street, through applauding crowds.
The citizens were not " with terror dumb " after
we got there.   By noon we reached the line of
works at Fort Stevens and found a rattled lot of
defenders, brave enough, but with no coherence
or organization.   Within the forts there were
plenty of brigadier-generals with new shoulder
straps wandering proudly about, the treasury
guards pale with anticipated battle, the quarter-
masters and commissary men, reserve batteries,

all war's motley ; and without, as fine a corps of
infantry as ever marched to tap of drum were
closing in upon the Capitol, with the stars and
bars waving.

I was sitting on the rampart of Fort Stevens
watching our people get into position, and looking at the flight of shells from a few great guns
firing, when I saw the President standing on the
wall a little way off. Bullets were whizzing over
in a desultory manner, and the puffs of smoke
in the woods opposite were growing in number.
An officer standing on the wall between me and
Mr. Lincoln suddenly keeled over and was helped
away. Then a lot of people persuaded Mr.
Lincoln to get down out of range, which he very
reluctantly did. My attention was directed to a
movement of a little brigade out of the lines.
They moved forward so promptly and came into
line so cleanly that I wondered whose brigade
it was, but their colors were not visible from
where I sat. Had I known that it was my own
brigade, that the 7th Maine were in the first
line, I think I might have gone too, in spite of
staff duties. But a few more than a thousand
of them, and they are charging Early's corps!
The defenders of the lines look on in wonder,
the President and his party feel that a real
battle is before them at last, and we all hold our
breath as the two little lines strike the enemy.

Now they are wreathed in smoke of their own making, and the smoke clouds of the enemy float backward.

On they go through his line, while the fire crashes seem out of proportion to the fight. Back go the enemy, more we think from the sight of the 6th corps flags than from the number assailing them, and now the brigade are holding, in good position, a vantage ground in the rebel lines. Soon night is falling, column after column of the corps is pushing out beyond the fort, and the crackling skirmish fire only ceases with the darkness. The 3d brigade of Getty's division has smashed Early's line, and has lost every regimental commander. Back goes General Early that night, and Washington is safe again. Many of those who fell now lie in a little graveyard on the Seventh Street road. Few of the people of Washington since have recked for what they gave their lives. No knights in ancient tournament ever fought in prouder lists, or before a more honorable company, but the busy people of to-day have forgotten them.

> "Can storied urn or animated bust
>   Back to its mansion call the fleeting breath,
> Can Honor's voice provoke the silent dust,
>   Or flattery soothe the dull, cold ear of death?"

CHAPTER XXXVII.

" Comrades known in marches many,
Comrades tried in dangers many,
Comrades bound by memories many,
Brothers ever let us be.

"Wounds or sickness may divide us,
Marching orders may divide us,
But whatever fates betide us,
Brothers of the heart are we."

HALPINE.

AFTER the dreadful slaughter of Spottsylvania, when my regiment was left with sixty-five bayonets in line and in command of a captain, I thought it might be my duty to go back to it, so I asked the advice of General Patrick, the oldest regular officer in the field. His counsel was to remain upon the staff, on the ground that the regiment was then but a captain's command and that the highest use was in my present duties. After the fight at Washington, however, Major Jones of the 7th being killed and their numbers being some two hundred, I asked General Wright to be relieved from staff duty and returned to the regiment as we filed out of bivouac in a hot pursuit of Early towards Edward's Ferry. It seemed strange to be confined to the marching column again, and to see my late companions riding free in the distance, but regimental duty has its compensations; the hearty welcome of my hardy and gallant command, a large portion of whom had reënlisted for three years, was very cheering. My man Bennett welcomed any change, assuming the duties of caterer to our mess, and it is unnecessary to say we lived largely upon the country. He had a very small mule with two panniers containing cooking and table utensils, and when the time for the noon halt came, the mule was generally on hand, and duck, or chickens, or turkey, ready cooked, with apple-butter, honey, and other garnishings in plenty. Such luxuries were rarely available except in Maryland or the Shenandoah Valley. In Virginia, hard-tack fried in pork, with black coffee, was the bill of fare three times a day, if we were lucky enough to get it so often, and at times, when the herd got up, a very fresh steak was added. The colored people sometimes contributed a hoecake, and mutton occasionally varied our diet, as a little offering from the men. In no other mode of life could a pipe taste so good, especially around fires the nights in the mountains made necessary, while the distant bugles sounded the retreat, and where a soft bit of turf was soon to woo us to repose under the bright stars.

I forget in what campaign it was, but once I woke just before reveille and found myself covered with two inches of snow. The bivouac of a division of infantry was in sight, with the long stacks of muskets and what looked like little snow mounds as far as one could see. Then the fife and drum and answering bugles sounded reveille, and the wide, white plain turned black with men. The mounds burst asunder,

> "And the muttered sounds,
>   Changed into loud strange shouts and warlike clang,
>   As with freed feet at last the earthborn sprang
>   On to the tumbling earth, and the sunlight
>   Shone on bright arms clean ready for the fight."

We marched up the Potomac, forded the river near Ball's Bluff, pushed on to Snicker's Gap in the Alleghanies, then over into the promised land of the Shenandoah the 6th corps banners floated, into that land of plenty, but of humiliation, too, until Sheridan's army changed the record. Then back again to Washington in many a weary march, we in the line not knowing the reason why. When in Maryland again I heard the colonel was coming, was almost there; so when he hove in sight, I bade adieu to my little command and was soon reinstated at corps headquarters in the old duties. Then we pulled out again to Harper's Ferry, under Hunter, to repel a cavalry raid, but we could not

catch up with the cavalry. Through Harper's
Ferry, of giant mountains and sorry memories
and stifling, dusty heat, and soon back again into
the Maryland valleys, the column went; but at
last came Sheridan, and with him the hope that
some business was to be done. Nobody was hungry to fight, but we knew we were there for other
purposes than to be a traveling procession, and
the cause had been for a long time a failing one.
Even the thinking soldiers about their campfires
felt a discouragement the gloom of the Wilderness had failed to produce. Money was worth
about thirty cents on the dollar, but there was
small use for it with us. We did not see the
right kind of recruits coming to fill the little
regiments. Down the valley we went, now an
independent army, three corps and the cavalry;
Sheridan ubiquitous and gathering in our good
opinions fast. Colonel Tolles and Dr. Oehlenschlager of our staff were captured one day and
promptly murdered after surrender. This made
war look more serious than ever. Were we going back into barbarism?

As we started southward one lovely morning, expecting to reach Middletown, Arthur
McClellan and I rode ahead to try our good
horses and escape the dust of the crowd where
we were not especially needed. We supposed
our cavalry were in the advance. When we

reached Middletown, the girls, instead of making faces at us from the windows, seemed vastly pleased about something, but this did not warn us. We rode on through the long straggling town, barked at by dogs, and laughed at by maids, till, near an old mill, by its farther bounds, we paused to look at the picturesque mountains, valleys, and streams, for which this part of the valley is renowned. Beyond was Fisher's Hill so soon to be famed in battle story; at its base far away a rebel regiment was drilling. The mountain air was keen, so we had light blue private's overcoats covering our uniforms. Suddenly rang out behind us the sharp challenge, " What regiment do you belong to ? " Turning, I saw six cavalrymen in dirty gray upon the road behind, carbines in hand. Their leader's jacket was slashed with gold, and a broad slouched hat shaded his face. As we turned, the buttons of our uniforms showed from our open overcoats, and the six carbines rang out in unison. Thoughts run rapidly in deadly emergency, and mine were, " What a wretched weapon," as the balls tore the old boards of the mill beside us. We cannot go forward, we cannot go back, so blessed be the lessons of our riding school on the banks of the Rappahannock, and blessed be our pride in having good horseflesh ! A half sideways jump over the fence to our right tests the mettle of our noble horses. In an instant we see the rebels cannot jump it. And then a race, we one side of the fence and they the other. They cannot load their carbines, and we pull our pistols from our boots and empty them gayly. Walls and fences are nothing to us. Soon we find their horses are not "in it," and in mad career free the town and leave our breathless pursuers. Thoughts of Tolles and of Oehlenschlager will not down at the bidding. Our winners in quarter mile races stood us in good stead that day. As it happened, our cavalry was not in front; these people were the rebel cavalry picket who chanced to be off for a while from the entrance of the town where they belonged, and hence the glee of the girls who saw us in the trap.

Then came a march up the valley to Harper's Ferry again, caused by the enemy getting in our rear. Night and day we went. One night about two o'clock, utterly weary, I thought I would go to the house of a doctor I knew, a Union man, in a little town, and catch two or three hours' sleep, and go along before the corps got by. I lay down on his parlor floor with a pile of music books for a pillow, and only was waked by the sun streaming in my face. Looking out of the window I saw seemingly interminable gray cavalry going by. My horse was in the barn adjacent, and I feared his whinny or other cause might attract some of them to the house. It was Mosby and his band following our track for stragglers. I was in what an Englishman would call a " blue funk," but could not help watching them, pistol in hand, till the last file went by. I did not dare till then to go after my horse, but when I did go, I struck a bee line for the mountains behind the town, and by twenty miles of devious paths in a hostile country, chanced to get to the corps again. These little adventures were heightened in excitement by a belief that capture would be followed by instant execution, and I think in the exasperated feeling of the day, it might have been so. As my time was out in two or three days, taking these chances was doubly unpleasant.

When we got back to the head of the valley, Early attacked us just as the 7th Maine were starting for home. I had bidden my friends a fond farewell, resumed command of the regiment, and started for the cars. We stopped for our share of the fight, which was a sharp one, till the Vermonters made one of their accustomed charges, ending the matter. Then off we marched, sadly leaving our reënlisted comrades, joyfully welcoming visions of home and of again seeing mother and sister, sweetheart or wife.

Soon mustered out, the career of the Seventh Maine Volunteers closed. Enlisted just after Bull Run, composed of people exasperated at our defeat, and going down to Virginia meaning business, it is little wonder they made a good record. Not once did they do anything the proudest infantry of this or any other time would be ashamed of. A lot of zealous, patriotic Maine boys, averaging somewhere about twenty-two years, they proved themselves worthy descendants of the farmer soldiers who held this border, the debatable ground, against savage and Frenchman, and who placed the English banners over Louisburg. Another generation of their ancestors assisted in nearly every battle of the Revolution, when from Kittery Point to Machias no draft or forced enlistment, but patriotism alone "robbed the cradle and the grave."

CHAPTER XXXVIII.

"Here Shenandoah brawls along,
There burly Blue Ridge echoes strong
To swell the Brigade's rousing song."

ANON.

IT was a long and hard journey from the
Shenandoah Valley to Maine in the war time.
We did not mind the slow trains and uncomfort-
able cars, however, for we knew no better, and
the anticipation of seeing family, friends, and
home produced a happiness that no outward
surroundings could lessen. The men who reenlisted for the war and those left behind had
been put into five companies, and two similar
companies of the 5th and three of the 6th Maine
joined with them, and it was rumored that the
intention was to call the organization so formed
the First Regiment of Maine Veteran Volunteers. What finer command could a young
soldier ask for? They were picked men, and
nearly all of them had been wounded in battle.
On reaching Augusta, I at once went to the governor and made application for the colonelcy.
He promptly said he had already determined to
give it to me. With my new commission in my

pocket, I bade a last good-by to the men who
were being mustered out, and then passed a few
days at the home I had several times supposed
I had visited for the last time. Newspaper
rumors of fighting in the valley caused another
start to the front. On reaching Washington, I
heard General Sheridan was at Willard's. Going to Willard's, I found he had just left for the
train; following him to the station, I found that
the train had just gone, and there was not
another till the morrow.

Ignorant that I was missing by a scratch
"Sheridan's ride," I took in review the brass-
buttoned patriots at the hotels, bought a pair of
colonel's shoulder straps, and carelessly passed
the time till the next day's train crawled slowly
into Martinsburg. The following morning I
procured a wretched animal of the quartermaster and a small escort of cavalry, for the twenty
miles to Winchester were said to be swarming
with guerrillas, and started out with many mis-
givings. The country looked about as Germany
may have looked after the Thirty Years' War,
but the scenery was all there. After a while I
found out that my cavalry were getting drunker
and drunker, and were useless but to attract
notice, so dismissing them, I kept on down the
pike on a steed that could not have run away if
he had tried to. All was stillness for fifteen

MAJOR C. A. WHITTIER, A. D. C.

miles ; it was the abomination of desolation, not even the "low of cattle and song of birds." Man was all there was to fear, however. At last, I saw calvary moving on the road far away, and when nearer saw a lady on horseback with an ambulance at their head, and soon had a kind greeting from Mrs. General Ricketts and from her wounded husband. They told me of the defeat and subsequent victory at Cedar Creek, how Sheridan had found the 6th corps undefeated and in line ready to advance, how General Bidwell had been killed at the head of my brigade, and many more things, and it dawned upon me that I had accidentally missed the opportunity of a lifetime for promotion. Pushing on to Winchester, I was received with the greatest hospitality by Colonel Edwards commanding there, and then spent the balance of the day in the hospitals, where it seemed as if I was finding everybody I knew.

Joining the brigade the day following, I found myself the ranking officer and in charge of it, so I never commanded the 1st Maine veterans. I found that regiment in an exceedingly unhappy condition. The old regiments that composed it would not mix at all and were jealous of each other in the extreme. By filling the vacancies in the 7th Maine companies by 5th and 6th Maine men and vice versa, it soon

became one of the most homogeneous organiza-
tions, as well as one of the best, I ever knew.
It was a proud thing for a boy to command a
brigade, and a good brigade too. There were
six regiments, and it happened the very first
afternoon that I had to take them out on brigade drill. I knew the tactics well enough and
got along finely at first, but at length I got
them by inversion and could not think how
to get them out. Major Long, their adjutant-
general all through the war, could or would not
tell me, so in a cold perspiration I marched
them up and down for a fifteen minutes that
seemed an hour, till the right order came to
mind.

The November days were beautiful, and the
nights cold in the valley, but our rude fireplaces
spread a cheerful glow by night as the autumnal
forests did by day. After Sheridan reviewed us
it came my turn to command the army picket
line. The enemy were threatening that day.
Our cavalry seemed to be coming back. Sheridan with a few officers passed through my line
out toward the firing, telling me to be in readiness for an attack, — and soon our people seemed
to be holding their own. That night I made
my headquarters at a house where there was a
large picket reserve, and lying on the parlor floor
with my sword for a pillow, trying to read by

the light of a tallow candle, I had just finished
the lines, —

> " Thou little knowest
> What he can bear, who born and nurst
> In Danger's paths has dared her worst,
> Upon whose ear the signal word
> Of strife and death is hourly breaking,
> Who sleeps with head upon the sword
> His fevered hand must grasp in waking,"

when volleys of musketry burst out from far
and near. Startled by them and by the coinci-
dence as well, I was soon in the saddle to see a
night attack repulsed.

We had dogs and double-barreled shotguns,
and as the country was full of rabbit, quail,
woodcock, and other game, our larders were well
supplied. Indeed, this portion of the valley was
a land flowing with milk and honey, and a proud
land too it remains in the memory of the 6th
corps. An uninterrupted series of victories had
perched on the banners of the Greek Cross, and
Sheridan, our greatest general, had said very
kind things of its devoted followers.

CHAPTER XXXIX.

"For men must work and women must weep,
The sooner it's over the sooner to sleep."
KINGSLEY.

ABOUT the 10th of December, 1864, Early's army having become practically extinct, we were ordered to the Army of the Potomac again near Petersburg. We took a train of box cars on the Baltimore & Ohio Railroad, and as it was cold weather and snowing hard, fires were built in the centre of each car on a platform of stones. At about ten miles an hour the brigade proceeded to Washington, where it was embarked on three steamers en route for the James River.

I took a smaller steamer for headquarters, and after going to see General Connor who was still in the hospital suffering from his wound received in The Wilderness, we steamed down the Potomac toward the dark and bloody ground about Petersburg. This time, however, there was hope in the air; all were beginning to feel that the next campaign would be the last, and most of the army now recognized the fact that emancipation had been the end for which the war had been permitted in the scheme of Providence. We landed at City Point, and while the brigade were preparing for a seventeen-mile march to our position in the line of the army, I called on General Patrick at Grant's headquarters. He asked me if I would accept the position of Provost-Marshal General of the Army of the Potomac, now vacant by reason of his going on Grant's staff, and said he had been asked to recommend an officer for that position. I pointed to my splendid brigade just moving up the road, and declined with his full approval, but it was pleasant to be so remembered by the old man, for whom I had always felt a lively affection.

The next day we went into camp on the Squirrel Level road, behind Fort Fisher, which made an angle in the line. The prospect was discouraging enough, the ground was swampy, the roads snow and mud. As we were likely to stay here three months, I set all hands at work draining the camp ground by a wide and deep trench, which the men called Dutch Gap Canal.

Then quarters were built on an approved plan, and it was not long before our camp was equal to any. At this stage of the war we had not only got to be quite proficient in utilizing all methods of cover from shot and shell, but had learned the value of hygiene, and paid as much attention to the health of the men as to their drill and discipline. If we had known how to

look after their health earlier, it might have
shortened the war.

This winter had very few excitements and a
great deal of very hard work. We had a brigade dress parade every afternoon at four o'clock
and went through the whole of the bayonet exercise to the sound of the bugle. Sometimes
the enemy attacked our pickets, inflicting loss,
but our orders were very strict about reprisals.
Deserters came in from the enemy in scores, and
their starved and wan appearance indicated better than anything else that the Confederacy was
on its last legs. From our picket lines, however,
we could see that the Army of Northern Virginia
was still a most formidable foe. Their forts,
with five lines of abattis in front, looked as if
they could defy any attack.

Generals Mackenzie, Warner, and I were
made a board of examination of officers for promotion, and this board, though a star chamber
and arbitrary in the extreme, was of great value
in that it could prevent poor officers being put
upon us by the governors of the States for political or other cause. One of my regiments was
commanded by a lieutenant - colonel who had
greatly distinguished himself and who had just
returned with an empty sleeve. This winter the
regiment got large enough by accession of drafted
men to allow a colonel to be mustered. The gov-

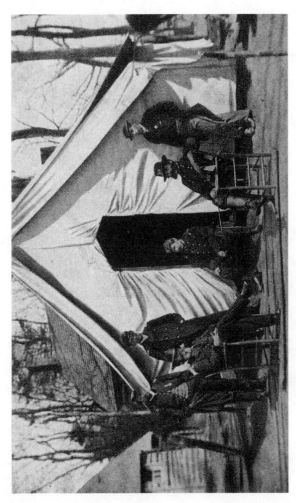

Gen. Schofield   Col. Whittier   Col. McMahon   Capt. Pierce
          Gen. Sedgwick   Gen. Getty

AT THE WELFORD HOUSE

ernor, paying no attention to the wishes of the regiment, or the recommendations of the generals of the army, that the lieutenant-colonel should be promoted, canceled some political debt by sending down a brand-new colonel. He arrived in the morning in spick and span uniform and very shiny equipment. At ten o'clock he went before this board, and the noon train carried him back toward his State again, a sadder and a wiser man.

By a piece of luck one day I discovered in one of the regiments a Frenchman who had been a cook in the Café Riche at Paris. We were not living very well, as the market was bad as well as our cookery, but when François took possession of the cook tent, it was another thing. I saw a genial and patriotic visitor of ours from Maine go out from one of his dinners entirely determined to give every man of the Army of the Potomac a dollar, and he kept on for quite a time too, till he realized how many of them there were.

We used to sleep with our clothes on against sudden attack. One night a dozen bullets ripped through the canvas roof of my house, and I succeeded in galloping out without any boots on, to find that they had made a swoop on our brigade picket, capturing about half of them. I sent Captain John Goldthwait, of the 1st Maine, to make a reconnaissance, and on his return he offered to take his company, with stockings over their boots, and, by crawling through an old rifle pit into their lines and getting behind their picket reserve, capture many more in return. He was a handsome fellow of rather melancholy mien, and he begged earnestly for the chance, telling me that he knew he should be killed in the opening battle of the campaign, and that he wanted to do something before he went. I started out promptly for permission in the morning, and it was approved till I got to General Meade, who as promptly refused. It was the only time I ever saw a presentiment realized. In our next battle, when I was obliged to sacrifice the 1st Maine veterans to save the brigade from being flanked, poor Goldthwait was almost the first man to fall, dying instantly.

CHAPTER XL.

"One crowded hour of glorious life
Is worth an age without a name."

SCOTT.

EARLY in the morning of March 25th, we were
awakened by tremendous firing far off to the
right. Every one was kept ready to fall in on
the instant, and after a while information came
that Gordon had attacked and taken our forts at
Hare's Hill. The rattling volleys and the cannonading kept on, however, till later information
told us that General Hartranft had succeeded in
driving him out. Then orders came to fall in,
and I felt that the time had at last come, so often longed for, when it should be settled whether
I could command six regiments in action to my
own satisfaction. It was an unknown problem,
a somewhat dreaded problem too. It was not a
question of danger at all, for in great responsibility, personal danger is little thought of by any
one. What is to be dreaded is, not doing the
right thing at the right time.

About noon orders came from division headquarters to "form the brigade in close column
of regiments behind the Vermonters, on the
right of Fort Fisher." Hardly was the brigade

in position when the Vermonters started forward toward the enemy's picket pits and forts, bending low to conceal themselves as much as possible, so the rebel cannon would not open any sooner than necessary.

I looked back over the brigade, and the picture still survives.   More than two thousand bronzed, hardy, and well-known faces, and every eye was upon me.   But it cannot be intended for us to follow the Vermonters merely to capture a few miserable pickets.   It is to take the forts, I reason, and wishing to get there as soon as anybody, I change the alignment of my first regiment so we can clear the Vermonters to their right, and off we go.   We are soon up with them.   Some thirty cannon open from the rebel forts to our right, to our left, and in front, but till we had captured and were by the enemy's pickets I don't think they hurt us much, as we were anything but a stationary mark.   Now half the distance to the forts is covered, and I look back to see Vermont is halted at the picket pits digging.

Forward my regiments were going in mad career; in their front the ground was flooded, and the only access to the forts was a narrow milldam not wide enough for two men abreast. Something had got to be done quickly.   It was perfectly evident we were not enough to get over there and hold anything, and also evident that

we were not expected to, so the recall was
sounded and the brigade got back and aligned
with the Vermonters before much damage was
done. The rebel cannon were worked for all
they were worth, but so far the balls were striking places we had just left. My right was in the
air, and from woods masking the rebel line to
our right a strong force bore down on that flank.
I at once refused the 1st Maine veterans and ordered the 122d New York in with them. Their
colonel, Dwight, had not time to obey the order,
as a shell took his head off, and I had to help
get them in place. Our fire was so effective that
the attacking force sought shelter in a large ravine from which no man attempted to emerge
for hours without being a target for many balls.
But the position of the 1st Maine was frightful.
There was an angle in the enemy's line off to
our left, so they were taken in rear by cannon,
enfiladed to their left by cannon, beside a front
fire. To change the range, I moved them as
often as possible to a new place in the same
general relation, that of protecting our flank, as
the enemy seemed to be reinforcing for another
attack. But the dreadful loss continued. I
saw a shell strike in a little picket pit containing three officers, and a foot, with boot and all,
flew over my head. I recognized then with pain
a mangled lieutenant of the 77th New York to

whom I was obliged a few days before to refuse a leave of absence.

As I was standing between the 77th and the 122d New York, a Vermont captain came up with his company, having become separated from his brigade, and asked for orders. At this moment I felt a bullet graze my arm through my overcoat, and saw the smoke of a musket from the roof of a large and comfortable-looking house between the lines. I ordered the captain to take his company and drive the rebels out, which he did in almost the time it takes to tell it, and returned to our line. But in a few minutes back the enemy came in greater numbers, and a dozen muskets flashed from the windows, now glistening in the setting sun. Again I sent the Vermont captain with orders to take and burn the house, which were promptly obeyed. All the while the cannoneers were working the thirty rebel cannon desperately. Still there was no movement of troops to cover our exposed right, and still all the signs pointed to an immediate attack from that direction. The whole situation was anxious in the extreme, when suddenly the 1st Maine rose to their feet and began to cheer. I could not see what for, so mounted and got to them at once, and to my delight and theirs the 1st brigade flag was pushing through the brush off to our right.

When this brigade got near enough for me to see Warner's happy face, delighted that his chance had come at last, I ordered the 122d New York and the 1st Maine forward at the double the moment that he was in line with us, and in a dashing charge we cleared the ravines for nearly half a mile, taking several hundred prisoners. But the darkness was falling, so we returned on the original rebel picket line and dug rifle pits, and my last waking recollection of that evening is a canteen of coffee my colored boy Bob brought after the cannon were silent and the glow-worm, like lanterns of those gathering in the fallen, were twinkling on the field. Why our batteries did not reply to the terrible fire from the Confederate forts is unknown to me. Perhaps they did, and, intensely occupied, I failed to notice it. So I had fought my brigade for the first time, and anxiety whether I had done the right thing kept off sleep that night.

In the morning a flag of truce brought a communication from General Cadmus Wilcox commanding the enemy, bitterly complaining of our vandalism in burning that house, which it seemed belonged to some one high in rebel circles. General Wright sent for me and ordered me to make a full investigation, but when I told him it was burned by my order and why, he had nothing to say, and what answer was made to General Wilcox I never heard.   While every one in the brigade was in this fight all I could ask, one of the most gallant pictures I recall is Captain Selkirk, inspector-general, on his gray horse, almost up to the opposite forts to bring back some of our men who either did not hear or would not mind the warning bugle.

When we got the Northern papers and looked eagerly for accounts of what we thought a pretty little fight, we saw: " There was heavy skirmishing on the lines of the 6th corps yesterday," and yet the losses of the brigade were more than those of the British army at Tel-el-kebir.

CHAPTER XLI.

"If Southern steel be sharp and keen
Is not ours strong and true ?
There may be danger in the deed
But there is honor too."

AYTOUN.

SHERIDAN had gone out to the left with the 5th corps, and orders came to us to prepare to make an assault on the works opposite, on April 2d before daybreak. General Wright came to my line to select a place to form the corps, and finally hit upon the left of Fort Fisher, where there was some rising ground behind our picket pits, and he chose a direction at a right angle to our attack of a week before. There was a right angle in the rebel line, as in ours, and there was no water in front of their forts on this side. The ground over which we were to charge had been burned over, and five formidable lines of abattis must be passed before reaching the fortifications. General Wright told me we would attack in a wedge-like formation, and that my brigade should be the point of the wedge. Some of our pickets that afternoon called my attention to an opening in the abattis through which our friends in butternut were accustomed to come out to cut wood and go on picket, and said they had noticed there was always a large camp-fire beyond the forts, that was in line with this opening, and that if we should direct ourselves on that fire we could get through the abattis easily. This is an illustration of the cleverness of the American private soldier. We would often hear from them criticisms of military movements and bright suggestions as they talked about their fires that would do credit to a trained staff. In the present instance it is probable that our assault was saved from disaster by this simple bit of information. As all details of the part the brigade was to take in the momentous battle of the morrow were left to me, I summoned the six regimental commanders and we went up a signal tower behind our camps, and with the heads of my discourse on the back of an envelope I have still preserved, and a copy of which is below, I delivered a lecture on what was to be done, and directed them to repeat the same to their officers, 1st and color sergeants.

1. Fall in at midnight.

2. Leave knapsacks and canteens in camp.

3. Load without capping.

4. File out to left of Fort Welch along ravine, and form as follows: —

43d N. Y., Milliken; 77th N. Y., Caw; 350 men.

1st Maine Vet., Fletcher, 350 men.

49th N. Y., Holt; 122d N. Y., Clapp; 400 men.

61st Penn., Crosby, 500 men.

5. Forty sharpened axes in front rank.

6. Signal to start, — a gun from Fort Fisher, one half hour before daybreak.

7. Guide on rebel camp - fire, over burnt ground and through openings in abattis.

8. When inside, keep right on and cut South-side R. R.

There was much to do that evening getting ready for what we then believed to be the final campaign. Our camps were to be broken up, all impediments sent to the rear, and everything needed for hard work got in order. A heavy mist made the moonless night more dark and gloomy, and the raw air of midnight saw us quietly moving to our allotted places. The rest of the corps was to our right and left rear in echelon of brigades formed in columns of regiments. The 3d division to our left was partly covered by a ravine. My first thought after getting the brigade in position was to look for the camp-fire that was to be our bright beacon, and there it was shining peacefully through the mist.

Our pickets had been strictly cautioned not to fire, but as we lay thickly packed on the rising ground behind them, some idiot fired his piece. The rebels promptly responded, and almost every shot they fired took effect in our column, as could be told by the thuds and stifled outcries. Captain Adams of Rhode Island then reported to me with twenty men of his battery carrying rammers and sponges, he having volunteered to go in with us to turn the enemy's guns on them as soon as taken. Then suddenly from all our forts to the rear burst the hail of shotted cannon. More than a hundred guns belched forth, and we learned that it was in honor of a great victory at Five Forks.

But in their clamor how was I to tell the signal gun for our advance? I started back to find out, and met General Getty, our division commander, who told me it was time to go in. I went over to notify General L. A. Grant, commanding the Vermont brigade next on our left, and lost a little time finding his successor, as I was told that Grant had just been carried off wounded by the wretched picket fire. Then standing on the rifle pits in front of the brigade I gave to each line of the column in as low a tone as possible the orders, "Attention! Forward! Charge!" and when conscious that the last line of black forms in the blacker darkness were over the pits, I followed as fast as possible, greatly regretting I had been so foolish as to have left my horse. I remember ordering a lot of rebels to the rear as we crossed their picket pits, for then the black darkness was becoming gray in the coming dawn, and the shot and shell from the enemy's forts were like so many rockets fired horizontally, and they were mostly a few feet over our heads. By their light, the trend of the attack seemed to be sweeping off to the right instead of going straight forward, and for a time I was swept that way, too, till I met Lieutenant Webber of the 1st Maine, who showed me our advance well up to the abattis. When we caught up with them they were resting a moment in the ditch, but they were soon over the works like so many cats, giving and receiving bayonet thrusts, and the cannon were hardly silent before they were fired the other way by Adams and his men.

It was now the half light of early morning, and from my horse, just brought up, I could see many of the brigade, each man for himself, pushing for the railroad; others dressed in Confederate officers' jackets were looting the camps; others were collecting droves of prisoners; others were on the mules of a captured train, and all about as happy a lot as could be imagined. As soon as word came that the track was torn up, the recall was sounded, and, forming with the rest of the division, we swept off to the left after the bulk of the enemy who had gone that way.

Piercing through the woods to a large clearing, we saw at its farther corner a few mounted men. A few shots — one of them fell, and was carried off by his companions. I have always believed that there fell General A. P. Hill, who was General Lee's right arm. When we reached Hatchers Run, Captain Merrill, of the 1st Maine, with 14 men, crossed it on fallen trees and captured and brought back 79 men, the sharpshooters of Heth's division. This shows how a night attack had demoralized our gallant foe. But the experience of this one would seem on the whole to condemn night attacks, for though it was successful and our loss was not serious, I think a very large proportion of those taking part in it got mixed up in the darkness and went the wrong way, and only the fact of our getting through the abattis so easily, gave us the victory. Of my six regimental commanders, Crosby and Holt were killed, Caw and Orr wounded; Caw by a bayonet. The 61st Pennsylvania had about 500 men that day: 200 of them old men, and 300 drafted men, substitutes, and the like. As we started the charge, the 300 of the latter disappeared and we never heard of them afterwards, but the 200 old men took two of the five colors captured by the brigade. The 200, in my opinion, should all have large pensions, and the 300 should all have been shot or hung. It would be

interesting to know how many of the latter lot in
after days turned up to be pensioned by a grate-
ful government, and still we wonder that the pen-
sion roll is not a roll of honor.

CHAPTER XLII.

"For the city is ours 'Mac' sought from the start,
An' our boys thro' its streets 'Hail, Columbia' are yellin';
And there's prayer in the air, an' there's pride in the heart,
And our flag has a fame that no tongue can be tellin'."

HALPINE.

AFTER reaching Hatcher's Run on the left, orders came to retrace our steps, and on getting back to the forts and camps we had taken, a brief halt was allowed for coffee. Here General Grant with a long cavalcade passed us and was cheered, and we saw the fine lines of battle of Ord's colored troops march over the breastworks we had won. Then the division was formed in line facing to the right toward Petersburg, the 3d brigade on the left, and I was directed to put the left regiment, the 1st Maine veterans, in echelon of companies to protect that flank. There was a good deal of firing off to the right where the 9th corps had not yet taken some forts, and to the left and front the enemy began to show themselves. As we advanced in a handsome line of battle over rolling and open country, our batteries galloped to the front and opened fire in a most spirited manner. But soon a rebel battery opened on our left almost

enfilading the line, and several times, as it was
forced to change position by the fire of the 1st
Maine, we noticed each time a fine-looking old
officer, on a gray horse, who seemed to be directing its movements.

At length the guns went into battery again
on a hill near a large house, and their audible
presence became more annoying than ever. By
common consent the three brigades attempted
to charge the hill, but the canister fire was so
hot and the division now so small and wearied,
the first attack was a failure. While our
men were getting in shape to charge again, I
sent Lieutenant Nichols with fifty men of the
1st Maine off to the left and around the hill
with orders to shoot the battery horses, as we
knew we could get on their flank, and they were
probably standing hitched to the caissons and
would be a fine mark from that side. As soon
as he had disappeared in a piece of woods, on
we started again. This time through a swamp
where many sank to the waist, and where shot
was splashing the mud and water in every direction.

Here I saw two color sergeants of the 1st
Maine fall, but the colors were picked up
promptly, and every one struggled over as best
he could, but the wounded, as well as the dead,
had to stay there for a time. The first five hun-

dred men across made a run for the battery, and
as we went up the hill amid the roar of guns
and whir of canister, amid Yankee cheers and
rebel yells, I detected the crack of Nichols's
rifles and knew the guns could not be got
away. The din was terrible! Brass Napoleons
were never better served, but they were doomed.
I saw Sergeant Highill of my brigade, General
Warner's orderly, and two Vermont colors go
between the guns at the same time, so neither
brigade could claim the sole honor. Riding
through the guns I could not see the road beyond where the enemy were retreating, for dust,
and most of the battery horses lay in their
tracks.

I asked a mortally wounded artillery officer
who was propped up against a limber what
battery it was. " Captain Williams of Pogue's
North Carolina battalion, " said he. " And
who was the officer on the gray horse," I continued. " General Robert E. Lee, sir, and he
was the last man to leave these guns," replied
he, almost exhausted by the effort. What a
prize we had missed! this gallant old man,
struggling like a Titan against defeat. He
had ordered his battery commander to die there,
and had done all one brave man could do to
save his fortunes from the wreck. They told us
the house had been his headquarters during the

siege of Petersburg. In a Confederate " Life of General Lee " I have seen this incident mentioned, but the account says he saved the battery.

As soon as our men had had a brief moment to take breath, we pushed on. The Appomattox came in sight, and more fire from across it. I sent Captain Whittlesey of the 1st Maine over on a hastily improvised raft, and his men soon scattered the discouraged foe. But off in the distance are the spires and inner works of Petersburg, and into them are double-quicking the gallant corps of Longstreet, called from the north side of the James too late to save the day. The sun is fast setting; Longstreet's force is vastly superior to our little division; we are halted while the Vermont skirmishers engage the new-comers, and we make the best line possible under the circumstances. General Penrose with the Jersey brigade comes up to relieve mine, and while I am telling him about what is in front of us, the last two shots are fired as the light is beginning to be dim. One kills Lieutenant Messer of Maine by my side, and the other knocks Penrose out of his saddle, though his belt plate saved him all but shock and pain.

Then we sink to the ground as we are; no supper, no blankets; nineteen hours of continuous marching and fighting has taken the energy

well out of everybody. We were too tired to
congratulate ourselves on the victory, and did
not care if Petersburg was in sight and near,
or grudge it to any one who would make the
capture. The next morning it surrendered to
our pickets, and Longstreet's glorious veterans
were far off in the race to escape.

CHAPTER XLIII.

"So sleeps the pride of former days,
  So glory's thrill is o'er,
And hearts that once beat high for praise
  Now feel that pulse no more."

MOORE.

WE were not destined to see Petersburg, before whose outlying fortifications we had stayed
so many weary months. I am not sure that it
was worth seeing from any point of view, but
I confess to a curiosity about the place, which
has not been gratified.

As the sun was beginning to put himself in
evidence, the drum beats called us from our
hard couches, and while the orders from division headquarters were being sent out, coffee
was served that seemed like nectar, though I
can hardly compare the hard-tack to ambrosia.
The orders meant a swift and sharp pursuit,
and they were obeyed. When we halted that
night after over twenty miles' progress, up came
our knapsacks in wagons jolting over stumps,
and in the round hole of the canvas at the end
of one was the warm-haired silhouette of my old
college friend, — so gifted, so loved, and soon so
sadly lost. Peace be to your memory, Moses

Owen! You did all you could to suppress the Rebellion in your laughing way. You cheered the warriors with quip and jest, and your songs were those of the bards of old.

On the morrow still another long tramp, through leafy woods and over rolling plains. Faint booming of cannon far away hurried our footsteps, and the desire to end the business with speed was in the hearts of each and all. And still pity and respect for the foe was slowly growing, as respect and camaraderie have been growing with us since many years toward our brave fellow countrymen who wore the gray.

The next day we were in line of battle, directed through a thick forest, toward Amelia Court House, as Lee was supposed to be there; but he was elsewhere, and the day following, in the forenoon as we were coughing in the dust, an order came back to double-quick, and the boom and rattling volley ahead gave token that we had caught up at last. On we went at the trot for half an hour, the toughest and bravest only being able to keep in the column.

My small brigade emerged from the woods to see a striking panorama unfold. On the left, Sheridan with his brilliant staff was fretting and fuming and raging that he could not do all himself, but yet happy that he had his favorite 6th corps with him at last; in front our 3d

GENERAL PHILIP H. SHERIDAN

division was charging over Sailor's Creek in fine array, upon a line of 10,000 rebels that might have seemed invincible, had we not seen beyond them the guidons of our cavalry as thick as flying leaves in autumn winds.

The smoke of burning trains made an horizon for the picture. I was proud to get the brigade into line under Sheridan's own eye, and in we plunged to take our part, but before we crossed the creek, which was choked with bodies and black with blood, the enemy, attacked from all directions, disintegrated, and many thousands threw down their arms. Lieutenant-General Ewell had yielded his sword.

Familiar and historic names by scores surrendered, and still some 1,000 of the Marine Brigade, formerly the Richmond Garrison, fought on. Beleaguered on all sides, it looked as if the fate of Cambronne and the old guard at Waterloo was theirs, but at last the arms were taken from their hands, as Custer's splendid cavalry were swooping down, following their gallant commander, his yellow locks floating in the wind. Here was near a third of Lee's army wiped out in one fell blow, and on we pushed in the forests for miles farther, though darkness did not come, for the rebel trains were burning.

Another day, and again the merciless tramp, with scarce a halt. Toward noon a sudden stillness came. The usual thunder around the horizon became strangely silent. It seemed as if we were marching in a vacuum. I dashed ahead to see what it meant, and within a mile came upon our revered division commander, General Getty, sitting under a tree, his face in his hands. "What is it, general?" "Lee has surrendered," was the reply. I joined him on the ground, and bitter tears fell for a career untimely nipped. Wicked, ill-timed, and selfish as it may have been, grief, that the glorious career of army life was cut short, was filling my boyish heart. Not enough developed to appreciate fully what this all meant to civilization, to freedom, and to countless generations yet to come, my own mistaken emotions must have vent for a moment. It was only a moment, however. I must tell the boys, and as I came back down the road at the pace only a Virginia running stallion can display, two thousand bright and eager faces were drawing near to meet me. "The war is over! Lee has surrendered!" I cry out, and am carried back and forth on stalwart shoulders. Discipline is at an end, and we are only patriotic American citizens for the rest of the day. The batteries fire off all of their cartridges blank, and the most crazy joy seizes all alike.

A great cavalcade is seen approaching us.

It is Meade followed by the generals and staffs of the army, a thousand strong. The men, 20 deep, line each side of his pathway and throw their caps and knapsacks under the feet of the horses. It is a saturnalia of joy, and not far away, happily unconscious of our ecstasies, the vanquished lion of the Confederacy and the remnant of his host are feeling

> " All the griefs that brave men feel,
> When conquered, e'en by foeman worthy of their steel. "

To our momentary disgust and to Grant's honor, we were, the next day, refused a sight of the Southern army. How mad we were, and how unjustly! We did not want to exult over them, but we were curious. The bummers, the sutlers, and all that would run the guard got over, but we were forbidden and would not try it. And they were spared what might have seemed to them a humiliation.

Only one Confederate officer did I see. Lieutenant-General Gordon came riding down the road by us like a knight of old. No better Southern soldier lived then or now. We can pardon the harm he did us, for his contribution to the American record for bravery and skill in arms.

CHAPTER XLIV.

"Farewell the plumed troops, and the big wars,
That make ambition virtue! Oh, farewell!"
SHAKESPEARE.

WE marched back to Burkesville junction, and late at night received the terrible news of Mr. Lincoln's assassination. Profound grief and indignation seized the army. Guards were doubled. No one knew what would come next; but the sober Yankee sense forbore reprisals and waited. It is better to lag in vengeance. One of the saddest sights I saw afterward was Mrs. Surratt in irons before her judges, and the court was composed of officers and gentlemen. The apotheosis of Lincoln was grand, but the country suffered under its great loss.

We were ordered to Sheridan, and the whole outfit was sent to finish Johnson in North Carolina. The marches were forced. My friends at headquarters started my little brigade out at daybreak to take Danville. We got there by noon. I sent a party over the Dan River by fords to the right, and while the mayor was surrendering at the bridge, had the place surrounded, and five thousand prisoners with some millions of property secured.

Then I was made military governor of the place and the three adjacent counties, and had the pleasure of being a satrap for a couple of months. My power was absolute; executive, legislative, and judicial, all were combined.

We began to parole our prisoners, and I remember taking account of 45 of them and 43 made their + mark. On entering the place, I saw the sign "Danville Register," and sent Moses Owen with orders to get out a paper. Jeff Davis's last proclamation was in type in the office when he got there. In a few hours, as the balance of the corps marched through, the newsboys were crying "The Daily Sixth Corps," and selling all that could be printed at 25 cents apiece. Moses took the owner of the paper into partnership, who never made so much money in his life. When Moses did not feel just right in the morning, he would publish the same paper as the day before, and it sold quite as well. His original poetry and imaginary dispatches from the North, as well as bulletins from the corps and personal allusions, make my files of the "Sixth Corps" unique in journalism.

The town was filled with Confederate officers, and we had no proper chance till I ordered all of them wearing uniform to report to the provost-marshal. Their uniforms were seen no more, and O fickle woman! the blue and brass buttons had then their legitimate field.   I think no citizen of Danville regretted our stay there, but the time came for us to be ordered North. We had heard of the Grand Review in Washington, and longed to be in it.

On a train that moved about ten miles an hour we started North.   Many urged me to burn the old rebel prisons as we went.   I should have winked at it, but the wind was toward the town, which forbade, as well as the attitude of the Danville people during our stay.   This was, as soon as they understood us, all that could be asked.

No incident, beyond running into a cow or two, occurred till we reached Richmond, when in as good form as we knew we passed the Spotswood Hotel, and saw war's ruin everywhere. It had taken four years to get there, and it was not much of a place after all.   The peaceful march to Washington over familiar war-worn ground seemed very queer.   There was no firing or the picket line at night.   We were all becoming impressed with the problem of what we were going to do when we got home.   The fellows that had stayed at home had all got a start, and we regarded our four years wasted for business purposes.   That was a mistake, however, for the discipline and subordination of the army had done us no harm, and if we did not do so well

as if we had had a longer apprenticeship, we
were docile and ready to work. The wonder of
the war was the sudden absorption of both
armies into the body politic again with scarcely
a ripple upon its surface.

When we got to Washington we had our own
review. It was phenomenally hot, even for
Washington. Behind the banners of the Greek
Cross some 12,000 hardy soldiers marched up
Pennsylvania Avenue, defiled before the President, and again sought the camps to speedily leave
them for their Northern homes. Many of us
were selected to form a corps for duty in the
South and against Maximilian, but the necessity
for it failed as time went on.

My last quasi-military service was serving as
marshal at the 4th of July celebration at home,
with orderlies, flags, and all. Then came citizen-
ship, and the record for some thirty years past
has told whether we were unfitted for it by the
four years of campaigning.

Should the flag again be threatened by civil
enemy or foreign foe, the survivors of the Great
War are not yet too old to be useful and will be
found, shoulder to shoulder with their old opponents, in defense of our common country, and
Liberty, the "Light of the world."

INDEX